The ETHICS *of*
Rhetoric

The ETHICS *of*
Rhetoric

By RICHARD M. WEAVER

ὥστε συμβαίνει τὴν ῥητορικὴν οἷον
παραφυές τι τῆς διαλεκτικῆς εἶναι καὶ
τῆς περὶ τὰ ἤθη πραγματείας

Thus it happens that rhetoric is an offshoot
of dialectic and also of ethical studies.

—ARISTOTLE, *Rhetoric*

Routledge
Taylor & Francis Group
New York   London

Routledge is an imprint of the
Taylor & Francis Group, an informa business

Published 1985 in the United States of America by Hermagoras Press, P.O. Box 1555, Davis, CA 95617. Originally published and copyrighted in 1953 by Regnery/Gateway Inc. (ISBN 0-89526-998-8). This edition manufactured in the United States of America with permission of Regnery/Gateway Inc.

Reprinted 2009 by Routledge

Routledge
Taylor and Francis Group
270 Madison Avenue
New York, NY 10016

Routledge
Taylor and Francis Group
2 Park Square
Milton Park, Abingdon
Oxon OX14 4RN

ISBN 10: 0-9611800-2-1   ISBN 13: 978-0-9611800-2-7

Table of Contents

Acknowledgments

ACKNOWLEDGMENTS with thanks are due the following: Charles Scribner's Sons for the passage from Allen Tate's "The Subway," from *Poems 1922–1947;* Karl Shapiro and Random House, Inc., for the passage from *Essay on Rime;* and the Viking Press, Inc., for the passage from Sherwood Anderson's *A Story Teller's Story.*

The ETHICS *of*
Rhetoric

Chapter I

THE *PHAEDRUS* AND THE NATURE
OF RHETORIC

OUR SUBJECT begins with the threshold difficulty of defining the question which Plato's *Phaedrus* was meant
to answer. Students of this justly celebrated dialogue
have felt uncertain of its unity of theme, and the tendency has
been to designate it broadly as a discussion of the ethical and
the beautiful. The explicit topics of the dialogue are, in order:
love, the soul, speechmaking, and the spoken and written
word, or what is generally termed by us "composition." The
development looks random, and some of the most interesting
passages appear *jeux d'esprit*. The richness of the literary art
diverts attention from the substance of the argument.

But a work of art which touches on many profound problems justifies more than one kind of reading. Our difficulty
with the *Phaedrus* may be that our interpretation has been too
literal and too topical. If we will bring to the reading of it even
a portion of that imagination which Plato habitually exercised,
we should perceive surely enough that it is consistently, and
from beginning to end, about one thing, which is the nature
of rhetoric.[1] Again, that point may have been missed because
most readers conceive rhetoric to be a system of artifice rather
than an idea,[2] and the *Phaedrus*, for all its apparent divagation,

1. Cf. A. E. Taylor, *Plato: the Man and his Work* (New York, 1936),
p. 300.
2. Cf. P. Albert Duhamel, "The Concept of Rhetoric as Effective
Expression," *Journal of the History of Ideas*, X, No. 3 (June, 1949),
344–56 *passim*.

keeps very close to a single idea. A study of its rhetorical structure, especially, may give us the insight which has been withheld, while making us feel anew that Plato possessed the deepest divining rod among the ancients.

For the imaginative interpretation which we shall now undertake, we have both general and specific warrant. First, it scarcely needs pointing out that a Socratic dialogue is in itself an example of transcendence. Beginning with something simple and topical, it passes to more general levels of application; and not infrequently, it must make the leap into allegory for the final utterance. This means, of course, that a Socratic dialogue may be about its subject implicitly as well as explicitly. The implicit rendering is usually through some kind of figuration because it is the nature of this meaning to be ineffable in any other way. It is necessary, therefore, to be alert for what takes place through the analogical mode.

Second, it is a matter of curious interest that a warning against literal reading occurs at an early stage of the *Phaedrus*. Here in the opening pages, appearing as if to set the key of the theme, comes an allusion to the myth of Boreas and Oreithyia. On the very spot where the dialogue begins, Boreas is said to have carried off the maiden. Does Socrates believe that this tale is really true? Or is he in favor of a scientific explanation of what the myth alleges? Athens had scientific experts, and the scientific explanation was that the north wind had pushed her off some rocks where she was playing with a companion. In this way the poetical story is provided with a factual basis. The answer of Socrates is that many tales are open to this kind of rationalization, but that the result is tedious and actually irrelevant. It is irrelevant because our chief concern is with the nature of the man, and it is beside the point to probe into such matters while we are yet ignorant of ourselves. The scientific criticism of Greek mythology, which may be likened to the scientific criticism of the myths of the Bible in our own day, produces at best "a boorish sort of wisdom (ἀγροίκῳ τινὶ σοφίᾳ)." It is a limitation to suppose that the truth of the story lies in its historicity. The "boorish sort of wisdom" seeks to supplant poetic allegation with fact, just as an archaeologist might look for the foundations of the Garden of Eden. But while this sort of search goes on the truth flies off, on wings of imagination, and is not recoverable until the searcher attains a higher level of pursuit. Socrates is satisfied with the parable, and we infer from numerous other passages that he believed that some things are best told by parable and some perhaps discoverable only by parable. Real investigation goes forward with the help of analogy. "Freud without Sophocles is unthinkable," a modern writer has said.[3]

With these precepts in mind, we turn to that part of the *Phaedrus* which has proved most puzzling: why is so much said about the absurd relationship of the lover and the non-lover? Socrates encounters Phaedrus outside the city wall. The latter has just come from hearing a discourse by Lysias which enchanted him with its eloquence. He is prevailed upon to repeat this discourse, and the two seek out a shady spot on the banks of the Ilissus. Now the discourse is remarkable because although it was "in a way, a love speech," its argument was that people should grant favors to non-lovers rather than to lovers. "This is just the clever thing about it," Phaedrus remarks. People are in the habit of preferring their lovers, but it is much more intelligent, as the argument of Lysias runs, to prefer a non-lover. Accordingly, the first major topic of the dialogue is a eulogy of the non-lover. The speech provides good subject matter for jesting on the part of Socrates, and looks like another exhibition of the childlike ingeniousness which gives the Greeks their charm. Is it merely a piece of literary trifling? Rather, it is Plato's dramatistic presentation of a major thesis. Beneath the surface of repartee and mock seriousness, he is asking whether we ought to prefer a neuter form of speech to the kind which is ever getting us aroused over things and provoking an expense of spirit.

---

3. James Blish, "Rituals on Ezra Pound," *Sewanee Review*, LVIII (Spring, 1950), 223.

Sophistications of theory cannot obscure the truth that there are but three ways for language to affect us. It can move us toward what is good; it can move us toward what is evil; or it can, in hypothetical third place, fail to move us at all.[4] Of course there are numberless degrees of effect under the first two heads, and the third, as will be shown, is an approximate rather than an absolute zero of effect. But any utterance is a major assumption of responsibility, and the assumption that one can avoid that responsibility by doing something to language itself is one of the chief considerations of the *Phaedrus*, just as it is of contemporary semantic theory. What Plato has succeeded in doing in this dialogue, whether by a remarkably effaced design, or unconsciously through the formal pressure of his conception, is to give us embodiments of the three types of discourse. These are respectively the non-lover, the evil lover, and the noble lover. We shall take up these figures in their sequence and show their relevance to the problem of language.

The eulogy of the non-lover in the speech of Lysias, as we hear it repeated to Socrates, stresses the fact that the non-lover follows a policy of enlightened self-interest. First of all, the non-lover does not neglect his affairs or commit extreme acts under the influence of passion. Since he acts from calculation, he never has occasion for remorse. No one ever says of him that he is not in his right mind, because all of his acts are within prudential bounds. The first point is, in sum, that the non-lover never sacrifices himself and therefore never feels the vexation which overtakes lovers when they recover from their passion and try to balance their pains with their profit. And the non-lover is constant whereas the lover is inconstant. The first argument then is that the non-lover demonstrates his superiority through prudence and objectivity. The second point of superiority found in non-lovers is that there are many

---

4. The various aesthetic approaches to language offer refinements of perception, but all of them can be finally subsumed under the first head above.

more of them. If one is limited in one's choice to one's lovers, the range is small; but as there are always more non-lovers than lovers, one has a better chance in choosing among many of finding something worthy of one's affection. A third point of superiority is that association with the non-lover does not excite public comment. If one is seen going about with the object of one's love, one is likely to provoke gossip; but when one is seen conversing with the non-lover, people merely realize that "everybody must converse with somebody." Therefore this kind of relationship does not affect one's public standing, and one is not disturbed by what the neighbors are saying. Finally, non-lovers are not jealous of one's associates. Accordingly they do not try to keep one from companions of intellect or wealth for fear that they may be outshone themselves. The lover, by contrast, tries to draw his beloved away from such companionship and so deprives him of improving associations. The argument is concluded with a generalization that one ought to grant favors not to the needy or the importunate, but to those who are able to repay. Such is the favorable account of the non-lover given by Lysias.

We must now observe how these points of superiority correspond to those of "semantically purified" speech. By "semantically purified speech" we mean the kind of speech approaching pure notation in the respect that it communicates abstract intelligence without impulsion. It is a simple instrumentality, showing no affection for the object of its symbolizing and incapable of inducing bias in the hearer. In its ideal conception, it would have less power to move than $2 + 2 = 4$, since it is generally admitted that mathematical equations may have the beauty of elegance, and hence are not above suspicion where beauty is suspect. But this neuter language will be an unqualified medium of transmission of meanings from mind to mind, and by virtue of its minds can remain in an unprejudiced relationship to the world and also to other minds.

Since the characteristic of this language is absence of anything like affection, it exhibits toward the thing being represented merely a sober fidelity, like that of the non-lover toward his companion. Instead of passion, it offers the serviceability of objectivity. Its "enlightened self-interest" takes the form of an unvarying accuracy and regularity in its symbolic references, most, if not all of which will be to verifiable data in the extramental world. Like a thrifty burgher, it has no romanticism about it; and it distrusts any departure from the literal and prosaic. The burgher has his feet on the ground; and similarly the language of pure notation has its point-by-point contact with objective reality. As Stuart Chase, one of its modern proponents, says in *The Tyranny of Words: "If we wish to understand the world and ourselves, it follows that we should use a language whose structure corresponds to physical structure"*[5] (italics his). So this language is married to the world, and its marital fidelity contrasts with the extravagances of other languages.

In second place, this language is far more "available." Whereas rhetorical language, or language which would persuade, must always be particularized to suit the occasion, drawing its effectiveness from many small nuances, a "utility" language is very general and one has no difficulty putting his meaning into it if he is satisfied with a paraphrase of that meaning. The 850 words recommended for Basic English, for example, are highly available in the sense that all native users of English have them instantly ready and learners of English can quickly acquire them. It soon becomes apparent, however, that the availability is a heavy tax upon all other qualities.

---

5. *The Tyranny of Words* (New York, 1938), p. 80. T. H. Huxley in *Lay Sermons* (New York, 1883), p. 112, outlined a noticeably similar ideal of scientific communication: "Therefore, the great business of the scientific teacher is, to imprint the fundamental, irrefragable facts of his science, not only by words upon the mind, but by sensible impressions upon the eye, and ear, and touch of the student in so complete a manner, that every term used, or law enunciated should afterwards call up vivid images of the particular structural, or other, facts which furnished the demonstration of the law, or illustration of the term."

Most of what we admire as energy and fullness tends to disappear when mere verbal counters are used. The conventional or public aspect of language can encroach upon the suggestive or symbolical aspect, until the naming is vague or blurred. In proportion as the medium is conventional in the widest sense and avoids all individualizing, personalizing, and heightening terms, it is common, and the commonness constitutes the negative virtue ascribed to the non-lover.

Finally, with reference to the third qualification of the non-lover, it is true that neuter language does not excite public opinion. This fact follows from its character outlined above. Rhetorical language on the other hand, for whatever purpose used, excites interest and with it either pleasure or alarm. People listen instinctively to the man whose speech betrays inclination. It does not matter what the inclination is toward, but we may say that the greater the degree of inclination, the greater the curiosity or response. Hence a "style" in speech always causes one to be a marked man, and the public may not be so much impressed—at least initially—by what the man is for or against as by the fact that he has a style. The way therefore to avoid public comment is to avoid the speech of affection and to use that of business, since, to echo the original proposition of Lysias, everybody knows that one must do business with others. From another standpoint, then, this is the language of prudence. These are the features which give neuter discourse an appeal to those who expect a scientific solution of human problems.

In summing up the trend of meaning, we note that Lysias has been praising a disinterested kind of relationship which avoids all excesses and irrationalities, all the dementia of love. It is a circumspect kind of relationship, which is preferred by all men who wish to do well in the world and avoid tempestuous courses. We have compared its detachment with the kind of abstraction to be found in scientific notation. But as an earnest of what is to come let us note, in taking leave of this part, that Phaedrus expresses admiration for the eloquence,

especially of diction, with which the suit of the non-lover has
been urged. This is our warning of the dilemma of the non-
lover.

Now we turn to the second major speech of the dialogue,
which is made by Socrates. Notwithstanding Phaedrus' enthu-
siastic praise, Socrates is dissatisfied with the speech of the
non-lover. He remembers having heard wiser things on the
subject and feels that he can make a speech on the same theme
"different from this and quite as good." After some playful
exchange, Socrates launches upon his own abuse of love, which
centers on the point that the lover is an exploiter. Love ($\epsilon \rho \omega s$)
is defined as the kind of desire which overcomes rational opin-
ion and moves toward the enjoyment of personal or bodily
beauty. The lover wishes to make the object of his passion as
pleasing to himself as possible; but to those possessed by this
frenzy, only that which is subject to their will is pleasant. Accordingly, everything which is opposed, or is equal or better,
the lover views with hostility. He naturally therefore tries to
make the beloved inferior to himself in every respect. He is
pleased if the beloved has intellectual limitations because they
have the effect of making him manageable. For a similar reason he tries to keep him away from all influences which might
"make a man of him," and of course the greatest of these is
divine philosophy. While he is working to keep him intellectually immature, he works also to keep him weak and effemi-
nate, with such harmful result that the beloved is unable to
play a man's part in crises. The lover is, moreover, jealous of
the possession of property because this gives the beloved an
independence which he does not wish him to have. Thus the
lover in exercising an unremitting compulsion over the beloved deprives him of all praiseworthy qualities, and this is the
price the beloved pays for accepting a lover who is "necessarily without reason." In brief, the lover is not motivated by
benevolence toward the beloved, but by selfish appetite; and
Socrates can aptly close with the quotation: "As wolves love
lambs, so lovers love their loves." The speech is on the single

theme of exploitation. It is important for us to keep in mind the object of love as here described, because another kind of love with a different object is later introduced into the dialogue, and we shall discuss the counterpart of each.

As we look now for the parallel in language, we find ourselves confronting the second of the three alternatives: speech which influences us in the direction of what is evil. This we shall call base rhetoric because its end is the exploitation which Socrates has been condemning. We find that base rhetoric hates that which is opposed, or is equal or better because all such things are impediments to its will, and in the last analysis it knows only its will. Truth is the stubborn, objective restraint which this will endeavors to overcome. Base rhetoric is therefore always trying to keep its objects from the support which personal courage, noble associations, and divine philosophy provide a man.

The base rhetorician, we may say, is a man who has yielded to the wrong aspects of existence. He has allowed himself to succumb to the sights and shows, to the physical pleasures which conspire against noble life. He knows that the only way he can get a following in his pursuits (and a following seems necessary to maximum enjoyment of the pursuits) is to work against the true understanding of his followers. Consequently the things which would elevate he keeps out of sight, and the things with which he surrounds his "beloved" are those which minister immediately to desire. The beloved is thus emasculated in understanding in order that the lover may have his way. Or as Socrates expresses it, the selfish lover contrives things so that the beloved will be "most agreeable to him and most harmful to himself."

Examples of this kind of contrivance occur on every hand in the impassioned language of journalism and political pleading. In the world of affairs which these seek to influence, the many are kept in a state of pupillage so that they will be most docile to their "lovers." The techniques of the base lover, especially as exemplified in modern journalism, would make a long catalogue, but in general it is accurate to say that he seeks to keep the understanding in a passive state by never permitting an honest examination of alternatives. Nothing is more feared by him than a true dialectic, for this not only endangers his favored alternative, but also gives the "beloved"—how clearly here are these the "lambs" of Socrates' figure—some training in intellectual independence. What he does therefore is dress up one alternative in all the cheap finery of immediate hopes and fears, knowing that if he can thus prevent a masculine exercise of imagination and will, he can have his way. By discussing only one side of an issue, by mentioning cause without consequence or consequence without cause, acts without agents or agents without agency,[6] he often successfully blocks definition and cause-and-effect reasoning. In this way his choices are arrayed in such meretricious images that one can quickly infer the juvenile mind which they would attract. Of course the base rhetorician today, with his vastly augmented power of propagation, has means of deluding which no ancient rhetor in forum or market place could have imagined.

Because Socrates has now made a speech against love, representing it as an evil, the non-lover seems to survive in estimation. We observe, however, that the non-lover, instead of being celebrated, is disposed of dialectically. "So, in a word, I say that the non-lover possesses all the advantages that are opposed to the disadvantages we found in the lover." This is not without bearing upon the subject matter of the important third speech, to which we now turn.

At this point in the dialogue, Socrates is warned by his monitory spirit that he has been engaging in a defamation of love despite the fact that love is a divinity. "If love is, as indeed he is, a god or something divine, he can be nothing evil; but the two speeches just now said that he was evil." These discourses were then an impiety—one representing non-love as admirable and the other attacking love as base. Socrates re-

---

6. That is, by mentioning only parts of the total situation.

solves to make amends, and the recantation which follows is one of the most elaborate developments in the Platonic system. The account of love which emerges from this new position may be summarized as follows.

Love is often censured as a form of madness, yet not all madness is evil. There is a madness which is simple degeneracy, but on the other hand there are kinds of madness which are really forms of inspiration, from which come the greatest gifts conferred on man. Prophecy is a kind of madness, and so too is poetry. "The poetry of the sane man vanishes into nothingness before that of the inspired madman." Mere sanity, which is of human origin, is inferior to that madness which is inspired by the gods and which is a condition for the highest kind of achievement. In this category goes the madness of the true lover. His is a generous state which confers blessings to the ignoring of self, whereas the conduct of the non-lover displays all the selfishness of business: "the affection of the non-lover, which is alloyed with mortal prudence and follows mortal and parsimonious rules of conduct will beget in the beloved soul the narrowness which common folk praise as virtue; it will cause the soul to be a wanderer upon the earth for nine thousand years and a fool below the earth at last." It is the vulgar who do not realize that the madness of the noble lover is an inspired madness because he has his thoughts turned toward a beauty of divine origin.

Now the attitude of the noble lover toward the beloved is in direct contrast with that of the evil lover, who, as we have seen, strives to possess and victimize the object of his affections. For once the noble lover has mastered the conflict within his own soul by conquering appetite and fixing his attention upon the intelligible and the divine, he conceives an exalted attitude toward the beloved. The noble lover now "follows the beloved in reverence and awe." So those who are filled with this kind of love "exhibit no jealousy or meanness toward the loved one, but endeavor by every means in their power to lead him to the likeness of the god whom they honor." Such is the conversion by which love turns from the exploitative to the creative.

Here it becomes necessary to bring our concepts together and to think of all speech having persuasive power as a kind of "love."[7] Thus, rhetorical speech is madness to the extent that it departs from the line which mere sanity lays down. There is always in its statement a kind of excess or deficiency which is immediately discernible when the test of simple realism is applied. Simple realism operates on a principle of equation or correspondence; one thing must match another, or, representation must tally with thing represented, like items in a tradesman's account. Any excess or deficiency on the part of the representation invokes the existence of the world of symbolism, which simple realism must deny. This explains why there is an immortal feud between men of business and the users of metaphor and metonymy, the poets and the rhetoricians.[8] The man of business, the narrow and parsimonious soul in the allusion of Socrates, desires a world which is a reliable materiality. But this the poet and rhetorician will never let him have, for each, with his own purpose, is trying to advance the borders of the imaginative world. A primrose by the river's brim will not remain that in the poet's account, but is promptly turned into something very much larger and something highly implicative. He who is accustomed to record the world with an abacus cannot follow these transfigurations; and indeed the very occurrence of them subtly undermines the premise of his business. It is the historic tendency of the tradesman, therefore, to confine passion to quite narrow channels so that it will not upset the decent business arrangements of the world. But if the poet, as the chief transformer of our picture of the world, is the peculiar enemy of this mentality, the rhet-

---

7. It is worth recalling that in the Christian New Testament, with its heavy Platonic influence, God is identified both with *logos*, "word, speech" (*John* 1:1); and with *agape*, "love" (*2 John* 4:8).

8. The users of metaphor and metonymy who are in the hire of businessmen of course constitute a special case.

orician is also hostile when practicing the kind of love proper to him. The "passion" in his speech is revolutionary, and it has a practical end.

We have now indicated the significance of the three types of lovers; but the remainder of the *Phaedrus* has much more to say about the nature of rhetoric, and we must return to one or more points to place our subject in a wider context. The problem of rhetoric which occupied Plato persistently, not only in the *Phaedrus* but also in other dialogues where this art is reviewed, may be best stated as a question: if truth alone is not sufficient to persuade men, what else remains that can be legitimately added? In one of the exchanges with Phaedrus, Socrates puts the question in the mouth of a personified Rhetoric: "I do not compel anyone to learn to speak without knowing the truth, but if my advice is of any value, he learns that first and then acquires me. So what I claim is this, that without my help the knowledge of the truth does not give the art of persuasion."

Now rhetoric as we have discussed it in relation to the lovers consists of truth plus its artful presentation, and for this reason it becomes necessary to say something more about the natural order of dialectic and rhetoric. In any general characterization rhetoric will include dialectic,[9] but for the study of method it is necessary to separate the two. Dialectic is a method of investigation whose object is the establishment of truth about doubtful propositions. Aristotle in the *Topics* gives a concise statement of its nature. "A dialectical problem is a subject of inquiry that contributes either to choice or avoidance, or to truth and knowledge, and that either by itself, or as a help to

---

9. Cf. 277 b: "A man must know the truth about all the particular things of which he speaks or writes, and must be able to define everything separately; then when he has defined them, he must know how to divide them by classes until further division is impossible; and in the same way he must understand the nature of the soul, must find out the class of speech adapted to each nature, and must arrange and adorn his discourse accordingly, offering to the complex soul elaborate and harmonious discourses, and simple talks to the simple soul."

the solution of some other such problem. It must, moreover, be something on which either people hold no opinion either way, or the masses hold a contrary opinion to the philosophers, or the philosophers to the masses, or each of them among themselves."[10] Plato is not perfectly clear about the distinction between positive and dialectical terms. In one passage[11] he contrasts the "positive" terms "iron" and "silver" with the "dialectical" terms "justice" and "goodness"; yet in other passages his "dialectical" terms seem to include categorizations of the external world. Thus Socrates indicates that distinguishing the horse from the ass is a dialectical operation;[12] and he tells us later that a good dialectician is able to divide things by classes "where the natural joints are" and will avoid breaking any part "after the manner of a bad carver."[13] Such, perhaps, is Aristotle's dialectic which contributes to truth and knowledge.

But there is a branch of dialectic which contributes to "choice or avoidance," and it is with this that rhetoric is regularly found joined. Generally speaking, this is a rhetoric involving questions of policy, and the dialectic which precedes it will determine not the application of positive terms but that of terms which are subject to the contingency of evaluation. Here dialectical inquiry will concern itself not with what is "iron" but with what is "good." It seeks to establish what belongs in the category of the "just" rather than what belongs in the genus *Canis*. As a general rule, simple object words such as "iron" and "house" have no connotations of policy, although it is frequently possible to give them these through speech situations in which there is added to their referential function a kind of impulse. We should have to interpret in this way "Fire!" or "Gold!" because these terms acquire something through intonation and relationship which places them in the class of evaluative expressions.

---

10. 104 b.
11. 263 a.
12. 260 b.
13. 265 a.

Any piece of persuasion, therefore, will contain as its first process a dialectic establishing terms which have to do with policy. Now a term of policy is essentially a term of motion, and here begins the congruence of rhetoric with the soul which underlies the speculation of the *Phaedrus*. In his myth of the charioteer, Socrates declares that every soul is immortal because "that which is ever moving is immortal." Motion, it would appear from this definition, is part of the soul's essence. And just because the soul is ever tending, positive or indifferent terms cannot partake of this congruence. But terms of tendency—goodness, justice, divinity, and the like—are terms of motion and therefore may be said to comport with the soul's essence. The soul's perception of goodness, justice, and divinity will depend upon its proper tendency, while at the same time contacts with these in discourse confirm and direct that tendency. The education of the soul is not a process of bringing it into correspondence with a physical structure like the external world, but rather a process of rightly affecting its motion. By this conception, a soul which is rightly affected calls that good which is good; but a soul which is wrongly turned calls that good which is evil. What Plato has prepared us to see is that the virtuous rhetorician, who is a lover of truth, has a soul of such movement that its dialectical perceptions are consonant with those of a divine mind. Or, in the language of more technical philosophy, this soul is aware of axiological systems which have ontic status. The good soul, consequently, will not urge a perversion of justice as justice in order to impose upon the commonwealth. Insofar as the soul has its impulse in the right direction, its definitions will agree with the true nature of intelligible things.

There is, then, no true rhetoric without dialectic, for the dialectic provides that basis of "high speculation about nature" without which rhetoric in the narrower sense has nothing to work upon. Yet, when the disputed terms have been established, we are at the limit of dialectic. How does the noble rhetorician proceed from this point on? That the clearest demonstration in terms of logical inclusion and exclusion often fails to win assent we hardly need state; therefore, to what does the rhetorician resort at this critical passage? It is the stage at which he passes from the logical to the analogical, or it is where figuration comes into rhetoric.

To look at this for a moment through a practical illustration, let us suppose that a speaker has convinced his listeners that his position is "true" as far as dialectical inquiry may be pushed. Now he sets about moving the listeners toward that position, but there is no way to move them except through the operation of analogy. The analogy proceeds by showing that the position being urged resembles or partakes of something greater and finer. It will be represented, in sum, as one of the steps leading toward ultimate good. Let us further suppose our speaker to be arguing for the payment of a just debt. The payment of the just debt is not itself justice, but the payment of this particular debt is one of the many things which would have to be done before this could be a completely just world. It is just, then, because it partakes of the ideal justice, or it is a small analogue of all justice (in practice it will be found that the rhetorician makes extensive use of synecdoche, whereby the small part is used as a vivid suggestion of the grandeur of the whole). It is by bringing out these resemblances that the good rhetorician leads those who listen in the direction of what is good. In effect, he performs a cure of souls by giving impulse, chiefly through figuration, toward an ideal good.

We now see the true rhetorician as a noble lover of the good, who works through dialectic and through poetic or analogical association. However he is compelled to modulate by the peculiar features of an occasion, this is his method.

It may not be superfluous to draw attention to the fact that what we have here outlined is the method of the *Phaedrus* itself. The dialectic appears in the dispute about love. The current thesis that love is praiseworthy is countered by the antithesis that love is blameworthy. This position is fully developed in the speech of Lysias and in the first speech of

Socrates. But this position is countered by a new thesis that after all love is praiseworthy because it is a divine thing. Of course, this is love on a higher level, or love re-defined. This is the regular process of transcendence which we have noted before. Now, having rescued love from the imputation of evil by excluding certain things from its definition, what does Socrates do? Quite in accordance with our analysis, he turns rhetorician. He tries to make this love as attractive as possible by bringing in the splendid figure of the charioteer.[14] In the narrower conception of this art, the allegory is the rhetoric, for it excites and fills us with desire for this kind of love, depicted with many terms having tendency toward the good. But in the broader conception the art must include also the dialectic, which succeeded in placing love in the category of divine things before filling our imaginations with attributes of divinity.[15] It is so regularly the method of Plato to follow a subtle analysis with a striking myth that it is not unreasonable to call him the master rhetorician. This goes far to explain why those who reject his philosophy sometimes remark his literary art with mingled admiration and annoyance.

The objection sometimes made that rhetoric cannot be used by a lover of truth because it indulges in "exaggerations" can be answered as follows. There is an exaggeration which is mere wantonness, and with this the true rhetorician has nothing to do. Such exaggeration is purely impressionistic in aim. Like caricature, whose only object is to amuse, it seizes upon any trait or aspect which could produce titillation and exploits this without conscience. If all rhetoric were like this, we should have to grant that rhetoricians are persons of very low responsibility and their art a disreputable one. But the rhetorician we have now defined is not interested in sensationalism.

The exaggeration which this rhetorician employs is not car-

---

14. In the passage extending from 246 a to 256 d.
15. Cf. 263 d ff.

icature but prophecy; and it would be a fair formulation to say
that true rhetoric is concerned with the potency of things. The
literalist, like the anti-poet described earlier, is troubled by
its failure to conform to a present reality. What he fails to appreciate is that potentiality is a mode of existence, and that all
prophecy is about the tendency of things. The discourse of the
noble rhetorician, accordingly, will be about real potentiality
or possible actuality, whereas that of the mere exaggerator is
about unreal potentiality. Naturally this distinction rests upon
a supposal that the rhetorician has insight, and we could not
defend him in the absence of that condition. But given insight, he has the duty to represent to us the as yet unactualized
future. It would be, for example, a misrepresentation of current facts but not of potential ones to talk about the joys of
peace in a time of war. During the Second World War, at the
depth of Britain's political and military disaster, Winston
Churchill likened the future of Europe to "broad sunlit uplands." Now if one had regard only for the hour, this was a
piece of mendacity such as the worst charlatans are found
committing; but if one took Churchill's premises and then
considered the potentiality, the picture was within bounds of
actualization. His "exaggeration" was that the defeat of the
enemy would place Europe in a position for long and peaceful progress. At the time the surface trends ran the other way;
the actuality was a valley of humiliation. Yet the hope which
transfigured this to "broad sunlit uplands" was not irresponsible, and we conclude by saying that the rhetorician talks
about both what exists simply and what exists by favor of human imagination and effort.[16]

---

16. Indeed, in this particular rhetorical duel we see the two types of
lovers opposed as clearly as illustration could desire. More than this, we
see the third type, the non-lover, committing his ignominious failure.
Britain and France had come to prefer as leaders the rhetoricless busi-
nessman type. And while they had thus emasculated themselves, there
appeared an evil lover to whom Europe all but succumbed before the
mistake was seen and rectified. For while the world must move, evil
rhetoric is of more force than no rhetoric at all; and Herr Hitler, employ-

This interest in actualization is a further distinction between pure dialectic and rhetoric. With its forecast of the actual possibility, rhetoric passes from mere scientific demonstration of an idea to its relation to prudential conduct. A dialectic must take place *in vacuo,* and the fact alone that it contains contraries leaves it an intellectual thing. Rhetoric, on the other hand, always espouses one of the contraries. This espousal is followed by some attempt at impingement upon actuality. That is why rhetoric, with its passion for the actual, is more complete than mere dialectic with its dry understanding. It is more complete on the premise than man is a creature of passion who must live out that passion in the world. Pure contemplation does not suffice for this end. As Jacques Maritain has expressed it: "love . . . is not directed at possibilities or pure essences; it is directed at what exists; one does not love possibilities, one loves that which exists or is destined to exist."[17] The complete man, then, is the "lover" added to the scientist; the rhetorician to the dialectician. Understanding followed by actualization seems to be the order of creation, and there is no need for the role of rhetoric to be misconceived.

The pure dialectician is left in the theoretical position of the non-lover, who can attain understanding but who cannot add impulse to truth. We are compelled to say "theoretical position" because it is by no means certain that in the world of actual speech the non-lover has more than a putative existence. We have seen previously that his speech would consist of strictly referential words which would serve only as des-

---

ing images which rested on no true dialectic, had persuaded multitudes that his order was the "new order," *i.e.,* the true potentiality. Britain was losing and could only lose until, reaching back in her traditional past, she found a voice which could match his accents with a truer grasp of the potentiality of things. Thus two men conspicuous for passion fought a contest for souls, which the nobler won. But the contest could have been lost by default.

17. "Action: the Perfection of Human Life," *Sewanee Review,* LVI (Winter, 1948), 3.

ignata. Now the question arises: at what point is motive to come into such language? Kenneth Burke in *A Grammar of Motives* has pointed to "the pattern of embarrassment behind the contemporary ideal of a language that will best promote good action by entirely eliminating the element of exhortation or command. Insofar as such a project succeeded, its terms would involve a narrowing of circumference to a point where the principle of personal action is eliminated from language, so that an act would follow from it only as a non-sequitur, a kind of humanitarian after-thought."[18]

The fault of this conception of language is that scientific intention turns out to be enclosed in artistic intention and not *vice versa*. Let us test this by taking as an example one of those "fact-finding committees" so favored by modern representative governments. A language in which all else is suppressed in favor of nuclear meanings would be an ideal instrumentality for the report of such a committee. But this committee, if it lived up to the ideal of its conception, would have to be followed by an "attitude-finding committee" to tell us what its explorations really mean. In real practice the fact-finding committee understands well enough that it is also an attitude-finding committee, and where it cannot show inclination through language of tendency, it usually manages to do so through selection and arrangement of the otherwise inarticulate facts. To recur here to the original situation in the dialogue, we recall that the eloquent Lysias, posing as a non-lover, had concealed designs upon Phaedrus, so that his fine speech was really a sheep's clothing. Socrates discerned in him a "peculiar craftiness." One must suspect the same today of many who ask us to place our faith in the neutrality of their discourse. We cannot deny that there are degrees of objectivity in the reference of speech. But this is not the same as an assurance that a vocabulary of reduced meanings will solve the problems of mankind. Many of those problems will have

---

18. *A Grammar of Motives* (New York, 1945), p. 90.

to be handled, as Socrates well knew, by the student of souls, who must primarily make use of the language of tendency. The soul is impulse, not simply cognition; and finally one's interest in rhetoric depends on how much poignancy one senses in existence.[19]

Rhetoric moves the soul with a movement which cannot finally be justified logically. It can only be valued analogically with reference to some supreme image. Therefore when the rhetorician encounters some soul "sinking beneath the double load of forgetfulness and vice" he seeks to re-animate it by holding up to its sight the order of presumptive goods. This order is necessarily a hierarchy leading up to the ultimate good. All of the terms in a rhetorical vocabulary are like links in a chain stretching up to some master link which transmits its influence down through the linkages. It is impossible to talk about rhetoric as effective expression without having as a term giving intelligibility to the whole discourse, the Good. Of course, inferior concepts of the Good may be and often are placed in this ultimate position; and there is nothing to keep a base lover from inverting the proper order and saying, "Evil, be thou my good." Yet the fact remains that in any piece of rhetorical discourse, one rhetorical term overcomes another rhetorical term only by being nearer to the term which stands ultimate. There is some ground for calling a rhetorical education necessarily an aristocratic education in that the rhetorician has to deal with an aristocracy of notions, to say nothing

19. Without rhetoric there seems no possibility of tragedy, and in turn, without the sense of tragedy, no possibility of taking an elevated view of life. The role of tragedy is to keep the human lot from being rendered as history. The cultivation of tragedy and a deep interest in the value-conferring power of language always occur together. The *Phaedrus*, the *Gorgias*, and the *Cratylus*, not to mention the works of many teachers of rhetoric, appear at the close of the great age of Greek tragedy. The Elizabethan age teemed with treatises on the use of language. The essentially tragic Christian view of life begins the long tradition of homiletics. Tragedy and the practice of rhetoric seem to find common sustenance in preoccupation with value, and then rhetoric follows as an analyzed art.

of supplementing his logical and pathetic proofs with an ethical proof.

All things considered, rhetoric, noble or base, is a great power in the world; and we note accordingly that at the center of the public life of every people there is a fierce struggle over who shall control the means of rhetorical propagation. Today we set up "offices of information," which like the sly lover in the dialogue, pose as non-lovers while pushing their suits. But there is no reason to despair over the fact that men will never give up seeking to influence one another. We would not desire it to be otherwise; neuter discourse is a false idol, to worship which is to commit the very offense for which Socrates made expiation in his second speech.

Since we want not emancipation from impulse but clarification of impulse, the duty of rhetoric is to bring together action and understanding into a whole that is greater than scientific perception.[20] The realization that just as no action is really indifferent, so no utterance is without its responsibility introduces, it is true, a certain strenuousity into life, produced by a consciousness that "nothing is lost." Yet this is preferable to that desolation which proceeds from an infinite dispersion or feeling of unaccountability. Even so, the choice between them is hardly ours to make; we did not create the order of things,

---

20. Cf. Maritain, *op. cit.*, pp. 3-4: "The truth of practical intellect is understood not as conformity to an extramental being but as conformity to a right desire; the end is no longer to know what is, but to bring into existence that which is not yet; further, the act of moral choice is so individualized, both by the singularity of the person from which it proceeds and the context of the contingent circumstances in which it takes place, that the practical judgment in which it is expressed and by which I declare to myself: this is what I must do, can be right only if, *hic et nunc*, the dynamism of my will is right, and tends towards the true goods of human life.

That is why practical wisdom, *prudentia*, is a virtue indivisibly moral and intellectual at the same time, and why, like the judgment of the conscience itself, it cannot be replaced by any sort of theoretical knowledge or science."

but being accountable for our impulses, we wish these to be just.

Thus when we finally divest rhetoric of all the notions of artifice which have grown up around it, we are left with something very much like Spinoza's "intellectual love of God." This is its essence and the *fons et origo* of its power. It is "intellectual" because, as we have previously seen, there is no honest rhetoric without a preceding dialectic. The kind of rhetoric which is justly condemned is utterance in support of a position before that position has been adjudicated with reference to the whole universe of discourse[21]—and of such the world always produces more than enough. It is "love" because it is something in addition to bare theoretical truth. That element in addition is a desire to bring truth into a kind of existence, or to give it an actuality to which theory is indifferent. Now what is to be said about our last expression, "of God"? Echoes of theological warfare will cause many to desire a substitute for this, and we should not object. As long as we have in ultimate place the highest good man can intuit, the relationship is made perfect. We shall be content with "intellectual love of the Good." It is still the intellectual love of good which causes the noble lover to desire not to devour his beloved but to shape him according to the gods as far as mortal power allows. So rhetoric at its truest seeks to perfect men by showing them better versions of themselves, links in that chain extending up toward the ideal, which only the intellect can apprehend and only the soul have affection for. This is the justified affection of which no one can be ashamed, and he who feels no influence of it is truly outside the communion of minds. Rhetoric appears, finally, as a means by which the impulse of the soul to be ever moving is redeemed.

It may be granted that in this essay we have gone some dis-

---

21. Socrates' criticism of the speech of Lysias (263 d ff.) is that the latter defended a position without having submitted it to the discipline of dialectic.

tance from the banks of the Ilissus. What began as a simple account of passion becomes by transcendence an allegory of all speech. No one would think of suggesting that Plato had in mind every application which has here been made, but that need not arise as an issue. The structure of the dialogue, the way in which the judgments about speech concentre, and especially the close association of the true, the beautiful, and the good, constitute a unity of implication. The central idea is that all speech, which is the means the gods have given man to express his soul, is a form of eros, in the proper interpretation of the word. With that truth the rhetorician will always be brought face to face as soon as he ventures beyond the consideration of mere artifice and device.

Chapter II

DIALECTIC AND RHETORIC AT DAYTON, TENNESSEE

W E HAVE maintained that dialectic and rhetoric are distinguishable stages of argumentation, although often they are not distinguished by the professional mind, to say nothing of the popular mind. Dialectic is that stage which defines the subject satisfactorily with regard to the *logos,* or the set of propositions making up some coherent universe of discourse; and we can therefore say that a dialectical position is established when its relation to an opposite has been made clear and it is thus rationally rather than empirically sustained. Despite the inconclusiveness of Plato on this subject, we shall say that facts are never dialectially determined—although they may be elaborated in a dialectical system—and that the urgency of facts is never a dialectical concern. For similar reasons Professor Adler, in his searching study of dialectic, maintains the position that "Facts, that is non-discursive elements, are never determinative of dialectic in a logical or intellectual sense...."[1]

What a successful dialectic secures for any position therefore, as we noted in the opening chapter, is not actuality but possibility; and what rhetoric thereafter accomplishes is to take any dialectically secured position (since positive positions, like the "position" that water freezes at 32°F., are not matters for rhetorical appeal) and show its relationship to the

---

1. Mortimer J. Adler, *Dialectic* (New York, 1927), p. 75.

world of prudential conduct. This is tantamount to saying that what the specifically rhetorical plea asks of us is belief, which is a preliminary to action.

It may be helpful to state this relationship through an example less complex than that of the Platonic dialogue. The speaker who in a dialectical contest has taken the position that "magnanimity is a virtue" has by his process of opposition and exclusion won our intellectual assent, inasmuch as we see the abstract possibility of this position in the world of discourse. He has not, however, produced in us a resolve to practice magnanimity. To accomplish this he must pass from the realm of possibility to that of actuality; it is not the logical invincibility of "magnanimity" enclosed in the class "virtue" which wins our assent; rather it is the contemplation of magnanimity *sub specie* actuality. Accordingly when we say that rhetoric instills belief and action, we are saying that it intersects possibility with the plane of actuality and hence of the imperative.[2]

A failure to appreciate this distinction is responsible for many lame performances in our public controversies. The effects are, in outline, that the dialectician cannot understand why his demonstration does not win converts; and the rhetorician cannot understand why his appeal is rejected as specious. The answer, as we have begun to indicate, is that the dialectic has not made reference to reality, which men confronted with problems of conduct require; and the rhetorician has not searched the grounds of the position on which he has perhaps spent much eloquence. True, the dialectician and the rhetorician are often one man, and the two processes may not lie apart in his work; but no student of the art of argumenta-

2. Cf. Adler, *op. cit.*, pp. 243–44: Dialectic "is a kind of thinking which satisfies these two values: in the essential inconclusiveness of its process, it avoids ever resting in belief, or in the assertion of truth; through its utter restriction to the universe of discourse and its disregard for whatever reference discourse may have toward actuality, it is barren of any practical issue. It can make no difference in the way of conduct."

tion can doubt that some extraordinary confusions would be prevented by a knowledge of the theory of this distinction. Beyond this, representative government would receive a tonic effect from any improvement of the ability of an electorate to distinguish logical positions from the detail of rhetorical amplification. The British, through their custom of putting questions to public speakers and to officers of government in Parliament, probably come nearest to getting some dialectical clarification from their public figures. In the United States, where there is no such custom, it is up to each disputant to force the other to reveal his grounds; and this, in the ardor of shoring up his own position rhetorically, he often fails to do with any thoroughness. It should therefore be profitable to try the kind of analysis we have explained upon some celebrated public controversy, with the object of showing how such grasp of rhetorical theory could have made the issues clearer.

For this purpose, it would be hard to think of a better example than the Scopes "evolution" trial of a generation ago. There is no denying that this trial had many aspects of the farcical, and it might seem at first glance not serious enough to warrant this type of examination. Yet at the time it was considered serious enough to draw the most celebrated trial lawyers of the country, as well as some of the most eminent scientists; moreover, after one has cut through the sensationalism with which journalism and a few of the principals clothed the encounter, one finds a unique alignment of dialectical and rhetorical positions.

The background of the trial can be narrated briefly. On March 21, 1925, the state of Tennessee passed a law forbidding the teaching of the theory of evolution in publicly supported schools. The language of the law was as follows:

Section 1. Be it enacted by the general assembly of the state of Tennessee, that it shall be unlawful for any teacher in any of the universities, normals and all other public schools of the state, which are supported in whole or in part by the public school funds of the state, to teach any theory that denies the story of the Divine creation of man as taught in the Bible, and to teach instead that man has descended from a lower order of animals.

That same spring John T. Scopes, a young instructor in biology in the high school at Dayton, made an agreement with some local citizens to teach such a theory and to cause himself to be indicted therefor with the object of testing the validity of the law. The indictment was duly returned, and the two sides prepared for the contest. The issue excited the nation as a whole; and the trial drew as opposing counsel Clarence Darrow, the celebrated Chicago lawyer, and William Jennings Bryan, the former political leader and evangelical lecturer.

The remarkable aspect of this trial was that almost from the first the defense, pleading the cause of science, was forced into the role of rhetorician; whereas the prosecution, pleading the cause of the state, clung stubbornly to a dialectical position. This development occurred because the argument of the defense, once the legal technicalities were got over, was that evolution is "true." The argument of the prosecution was that its teaching was unlawful. These two arguments depend upon rhetoric and dialectic respectively. Because of this circumstance, the famous trial turned into an argument about the orders of knowledge, although this fact was never clearly expressed, if it was ever discerned, by either side, and that is the main subject of our analysis. But before going into the matter of the trial, a slight prologue may be in order.

It is only the first step beyond philosophic naïvete to realize that there are different orders of knowledge, or that not all knowledge is of the same kind of thing. Adler, whose analysis I am satisfied to accept to some extent, distinguishes the orders as follows. First there is the order of facts about existing physical entities. These constitute the simple data of science. Next come the statements which are statements about these facts; these are the propositions or theories of science. Next there come the statements about these statements: "The propositions which these last statements express form a partial universe of discourse which is the body of philosophical opinion."[3]

To illustrate in sequence: the anatomical measurements of *Pithecanthropus erectus* would be knowledge of the first order. A theory based on these measurements which placed him in a certain group of related organisms would be knowledge of the second order. A statement about the value or the implications of the theory of this placement would be knowledge of the third order; it would be the judgment of a scientific theory from a dialectical position.

It is at once apparent that the Tennessee "anti-evolution" law was a statement of the third class. That is to say, it was neither a collection of scientific facts, nor a statement about those facts (*i.e.*, a theory or a generalization); it was a statement about a statement (the scientists' statement) purporting to be based on those facts. It was, to use Adler's phrase, a philosophical opinion, though expressed in the language of law. Now since the body of philosophical opinion is on a level which surmounts the partial universe of science, how is it possible for the latter ever to refute the former? In short, is there any number of facts, together with generalizations based on facts, which would be sufficient to overcome a dialectical position?

Throughout the trial the defense tended to take the view that science could carry the day just by being scientific. But in doing this, one assumes that there are no points outside the empirical realm from which one can form judgments about science. Science, by this conception, must contain not only its facts, but also the means of its own evaluation, so that the statements about the statements of science are science too.

The published record of the trial runs to approximately

---

3. Adler, *op. cit.*, p. 224.

three hundred pages, and it would obviously be difficult to present a digest of all that was said. But through a carefully selected series of excerpts, it may be possible to show how blows were traded back and forth from the two positions. The following passages, though not continuous, afford the clearest picture of the dialectical-rhetorical conflict which underlay the entire trial.

THE COURT (*in charging the grand jury*)

You will bear in mind that in this investigation you are not interested to inquire into the policy of this legislation.[4]

THE PROSECUTION

Attorney-General Stewart: If the Court please, in this case, as Mr. Darrow stated, the defense is going to insist on introducing scientists and Bible students to give their ideas on certain views of this law, and that, I am frank to state, will be resisted by the state as vigorously as we know

THE DEFENSE

Mr. Darrow: I don't suppose the court has considered the question of competency of evidence. My associates and myself have fairly definite ideas as to it, but I don't know how the counsel on the other side feel about it. I think that scientists are competent evidence—or competent witnesses here, to explain what evolution is, and that they are competent on both sides.

4. All quotations are given verbatim from *The World's Most Famous Court Trial* (National Book Company, Cincinnati, 1925), a complete transcript.

THE PROSECUTION

how to resist it. We have had a conference or two about the matter, and we think that it isn't competent evidence; that is, it is not competent to bring into this case scientists who testify as to what the theory of evolution is or interpret the Bible or anything of that sort.

Mr. McKenzie: Under the law you cannot teach in the common schools the Bible. Why should it be improper to provide that you cannot teach this other theory?

THE DEFENSE

Mr. Neal: The defendant moves the court to quash the indictment in this case for the following reasons: In that it violates Sec. 12, Art. XI, of the Constitution of Tennessee: "It shall be the duty of the general assembly in all future periods of the government to cherish literature and science. . . . I want to say that our main contention after all, may it please your honor, is that this is not a proper thing for any legislature, the legislature of Tennessee or the legislature of the United States, to attempt to make and assign a rule in regard to. In this law there is an attempt to pronounce a judgment and a conclusion in the realm of science and in the realm of religion.

THE PROSECUTION   THE DEFENSE

Mr. Darrow: Can a legislative
body say, "You cannot read a
book or take a lesson or make a
talk on science until you first
find out whether you are saying
against Genesis"? It can unless
that constitutional provision
protects me. It can. Can it say
to the astronomer, you cannot
turn your telescope upon the infinite planets and suns and stars
that fill space, lest you find that
the earth is not the center of the
universe and that there is not
any firmament between us and
the heaven? Can it? It could—
except for the work of Thomas
Jefferson, which has been wov-
en into every state constitution
in the Union, and has stayed
there like a flaming sword to
protect the rights of man against
ignorance and bigotry, and
when it is permitted to over-
whelm them then we are taken
in a sea of blood and ruin that
all the miseries and tortures and
carrion of the middle ages
would be as nothing. . . . If today you can take a thing like
evolution and make it a crime
to teach it in the public schools,
tomorrow you can make it a
crime to teach it in the private
schools, and the next year you
can make it a crime to teach it
to the hustings or in the church.

THE PROSECUTION

THE DEFENSE

At the next session you may ban books and the newspapers.

Mr. Dudley Field Malone: So that there shall be no misunderstanding and that no one shall be able to misinterpret or misrepresent our position we wish to state at the beginning of the case that the defense believes that there is a direct conflict between the theory of evolution and the theories of creation as set forth in the Book of Genesis.

Neither do we believe that the stories of creation as set forth in the Bible are reconcilable or scientifically correct.

Mr. Arthur Garfield Hays: Our whole case depends upon proving that evolution is a reasonable scientific theory.

Mr. William Jennings Bryan, Jr. (in support of a motion to exclude expert testimony): It is, I think, apparent to all that we have now reached the heart of this case, upon your honor's ruling, as to whether this expert testimony will be admitted largely determines the question of whether this trial from now on will be an orderly effort to try the case upon the issues, raised by the indictment and by the plea or whether it will degenerate into a joint debate upon the merits or demerits of someone's views upon evolution. . . . To permit an expert to testify upon this issue would be to substitute trial by experts for trial by jury. . . .

Mr. William Jennings Bryan: An expert cannot be permitted to come in here and try to defeat the enforcement of a law by testifying that it isn't a bad law and it isn't—I mean a bad doctrine—no matter how these people phrase the doctrine—no matter how they eulogize it. This is not the place to prove that the law ought never to have been passed. The place to prove that, or teach that, was to the state legislature. . . . The people of this state passed this law, the people of the state knew what they were doing when they passed the law, and they knew the dangers of the doctrine— that they did not want it taught to their children, and my friends, it isn't—your honor, it isn't proper to bring experts in here and try to defeat the purpose of the people of this state by try-

Mr. Hays: Are we entitled to show what evolution is? We are entitled to show that, if for no other reason than to determine whether the title is germane to the act.

ing to show that this thing they
denounce and outlaw is a beautiful thing that everybody ought
to believe in. . . . It is this doctrine that gives us Nietzsche, the
only great author who tried to
carry this to its logical conclusion, and we have the testimony
of my distinguished friend from
Chicago in his speech in the
Loeb and Leopold case that 50,-
000 volumes have been written
about Nietzsche, and he is the
greatest philosopher in the last
hundred years, and have him
pleading that because Leopold
read Nietzsche and adopted Nietzsche's philosophy of the super-
man, that he is not responsible
for the taking of human life. We
have the doctrine—I should not
characterize it as I should like
to characterize it—the doctrine
that the universities that had it
taught, and the professors who
taught it, are much more responsible for the crime that Leopold committed than Leopold
himself. That is the doctrine,
my friends, that they have tried
to bring into existence, they
commence in the high schools
with their foundation of evolutionary theory, and we have the
word of the distinguished lawyer that this is more read than
any other in a hundred years,

THE PROSECUTION   THE DEFENSE

and the statement of that distinguished man that the teachings of Nietzsche made Leopold
a murderer. . . . (*Mr. Bryan
reading from a book by Darrow*) "I will guarantee that you
can go to the University of Chicago today—into its big library
and find over 1,000 volumes of
Nietzsche, and I am sure I speak
moderately. If this boy is to
blame for this, where did he get
it? Is there any blame attached
because somebody took Nietzsche's philosophy seriously and
fashioned his life on it? And
there is no question in this case
but what it is true. Then who is
to blame? The university would
be more to blame than he is. The
scholars of the world would be
more to blame than he is. The
publishers of the world—and
Nietzsche's books are published
by one of the biggest publishers
in the world—are more to blame
than he is. Your honor, it is
hardly fair to hang a 19-year-old
boy for the philosophy that was
taught him at the university."
. . . Your honor, we first pointed
out that we do not need any experts in science. Here is one
plain fact, and the statute defines itself, and it tells the kind
of evolution it does not want
taught, and the evidence says

The Prosecution

that this is the kind of evolution that was taught, and no number of scientists could come in here, my friends, and override that statute or take from the jury its right to decide this question, so that all the experts they could bring would mean nothing. And when it comes to Bible experts, every member of the jury is as good an expert on the Bible as any man they could bring, or that we could bring.

Mr. Stewart: Now what could these scientists testify to? They could only say as an expert, qualified as an expert upon this subject, I have made a study of these things and from my standpoint as such an expert, I say that this does not deny the story of divine creation. That is what they would testify to, isn't it?

The Defense

Mr. Malone: Are we to have our children know nothing about science except what the church says they shall know? I have never seen any harm in learning and understanding, in humility and open-mindedness, and I have never seen clearer the need of that learning than when I see the attitude of the prosecution, who attack and refuse to accept the information and intelligence, which expert witnesses will give them.

THE PROSECUTION

That is all they could testify about.

Now, then, I say under the correct construction of the act, that they cannot testify as to that. Why? Because in the wording of this act the legislature itself construed the instrument according to their intention. . . . What was the general purpose of the legislature here? It was to prevent teaching in the public schools of any county in Tennessee that theory which says that man is descended from a lower order of animals. That is the intent and nobody can dispute it under the shining sun of this day.

THE DEFENSE

THE COURT

Now upon these issues as brought up it becomes the duty of the Court to determine the question of the admissibility of this expert testimony offered by the defendant.

It is not within the province of the Court under these issues to decide and determine which is true, the story of divine creation as taught in the Bible, or the story of the creation of man as taught by evolution.

If the state is correct in its insistence, it is immaterial, so far as the results of this case are concerned, as to which theory is true; because it is within the province of the legislative branch, and not the judicial branch of the government to pass upon the policy of a statute; and the policy of this statute having been passed upon by that department of the government, this court is not further concerned as to its policy; but is interested only in its proper interpretation and, if valid, its enforcement. . . . Therefore the court is content to sustain the motion of the attorney-general to exclude expert testimony.

THE PROSECUTION	THE DEFENSE

Mr. Stewart (during Mr. Darrow's cross-examination of Mr. Bryan): I want to interpose another objection. What is the purpose of this examination?

Mr. Bryan: The purpose is to cast ridicule upon everybody who believes in the Bible, and I am perfectly willing that the world shall know that these gentlemen have no other purpose than ridiculing every Christian who believes in the Bible.

Mr. Darrow: We have the purpose of preventing bigots and ignoramuses from controlling the education of the United States, and you know it, and that is all.

Statements of Noted Scientists as Filed into Record by Defense Counsel

Charles H. Judd, Director of School of Education, University of Chicago: It will be impossible, in my judgment, in the state university, as well as in the normal schools, to teach adequately psychology or the science of education without making constant reference to all the

THE PROSECUTION

THE DEFENSE

facts of mental development which are included in the general doctrine of evolution. . . . Whatever may be the constitutional rights of legislatures to prescribe the general course of study of public schools it will, in my judgment, be a serious national disaster if the attempt is successful to determine the details to be taught in the schools through the vote of legislatures rather than as a result of scientific investigation.

Jacob G. Lipman, Dean of the College of Agriculture, State University of New Jersey: With these facts and interpretations of organic evolution left out, the agricultural colleges and experimental stations could not render effective service to our great agricultural industry.

Wilbur A. Nelson, State Geologist of Tennessee: It, therefore, apears that it would be impossible to study or teach geology in Tennessee or elsewhere, without using the theory of evolution.

Kirtley F. Mather, Chairman of the Department of Geology, Harvard University: Science has not even a guess as to the original source or sources of matter.

THE PROSECUTION   THE DEFENSE

It deals with immediate causes and effects. . . . Men of science have as their aim the discovery of facts. They seek with open eyes, willing to recognize it, as Huxley said, even if it "sears the eyeballs." After they have discovered truth, and not till then, do they consider what its moral implications may be. Thus far, and presumably always, truth when found is also found to be right, in the moral sense of the word. . . . As Henry Ward Beecher said, forty years ago, "If to reject God's revelation in the book is infidelity, what is it to reject God's revelation of himself in the structure of the whole globe?"

Maynard M. Metcalf, Research Specialist in Zoology, Johns Hopkins University: Intelligent teaching of biology or intelligent approach to any biological science is impossible if the established fact of evolution is omitted.

Horatio Hackett Newman, Professor of Zoology, University of Chicago: Evolution has been tried and tested in every conceivable way for considerably over half a century. Vast numbers of biological facts have been examined in the light of

THE PROSECUTION	THE DEFENSE
	this principle and without a single exception they have been entirely compatible with it. . . . The evolution principle is thus a great unifying and integrating scientific conception. Any conception that is so far-reaching, so consistent, and that has led to so much advance in the understanding of nature, is at least an extremely valuable idea and one not lightly to be cast aside in case it fails to agree with one's prejudices.

Thus the two sides lined up as dialectical truth and empirical fact. The state legislature of Tennessee, acting in its sovereign capacity, had passed a measure which made it unlawful to teach that man is connatural with the animals through asserting that he is descended from a "lower order" of them. (There was some sparring over the meaning of the technical language of the act, but this was the general consensus.) The legal question was whether John T. Scopes had violated the measure. The philosophical question, which was the real focus of interest, was the right of a state to make this prescription.

We have referred to the kind of truth which can be dialectically established, and here we must develop further the dialectical nature of the state's case. As long as it maintained this dialectical position, it did not have to go into the "factual" truth of evolution, despite the outcry from the other side. The following considerations, then, enter into this "dialectical" prosecution.

By definition the legislature is the supreme arbiter of education within the state. It is charged with the duty of promoting enlightenment and morality, and to these ends it may establish common schools, require attendance, and review curricula either by itself or through its agents. The state of Tennessee had exercised this kind of authority when it had forbidden the teaching of the Bible in the public schools. Now if the legislature could take a position that the publicly subsidized teaching of the Bible was socially undesirable, it could, from the same authority, take the same position with regard to a body of science. Some people might feel that the legislature was morally bound to encourage the propagation of the Bible, just as some of those participating in the trial seemed to think that it was morally bound to encourage the propagation of science. But here again the legislature is the highest tribunal, and no body of religious or scientific doctrine comes to it with a compulsive authority. In brief, both the Ten Commandments and the theory of evolution belonged in the class of things which it could elect or reject, depending on the systematic import of propositions underlying the philosophy of the state.

The policy of the anti-evolution law was the same type of policy which Darrow had by inference commended only a year earlier in the famous trial of Loeb and Leopold. This clash is perhaps the most direct in the Scopes case and deserves pointing out here. Darrow had served as defense counsel for the two brilliant university graduates who had conceived the idea of committing a murder as a kind of intellectual exploit, to prove that their powers of foresight and care could prevent detection. The essence of Darrow's plea at their trial was that the two young men could not be held culpable— at least in the degree the state claimed—because of the influences to which they had been exposed. They had been readers of a system of philosophy of allegedly anti-social tendency, and they were not to be blamed if they translated that philosophy into a sanction of their deed. The effect of this plea obviously was to transfer guilt from the two young men to society as a whole, acting through its laws, its schools, its publications, etc.

Now the key thing to be observed in this plea was that Darrow was not asking the jury to inspect the philosophy of Nietzsche for the purpose either of passing upon its internal consistency or its contact with reality. He was asking precisely what Bryan was asking of the jury at Dayton, namely that they take a strictly dialectical position outside it, viewing it as a partial universe of discourse with consequences which could be adjudged good or bad. The point to be especially noted is that Darrow did not raise the question of whether the philosophy of Nietzsche expresses necessary truth, or whether, let us say, it is essential to an understanding of the world. He was satisfied to point out that the state had not been a sufficiently vigilant guardian of the forces molding the character of its youth.

But the prosecution at Dayton could use this line of argument without change. If the philosophy of Nietzsche were sufficient to instigate young men to criminal actions, it might be claimed with even greater force that the philosophy of evolution, which in the popular mind equated man with the animals, would do the same. The state's dialectic here simply used one of Darrow's earlier definitions to place the anti-evolution law in a favorable or benevolent category. In sum: to Darrow's previous position that the doctrine of Nietzsche is capable of immoral influence, Bryan responded that the doctrine of evolution is likewise capable of immoral influence, and this of course was the dialectical countering of the defense's position in the trial.

There remains yet a third dialectical maneuver for the prosecution. On the second day of the trial Attorney-General Stewart, in reviewing the duties of the legislature, posed the following problem: "Supposing then that there should come within the minds of the people a conflict between literature and science. Then what would the legislature do? Wouldn't

they have to interpret?. . . . Wouldn't they have to interpret
their construction of this conflict which one should be recognized or higher or more in the public schools?"

This point was not exploited as fully as its importance might
seem to warrant; but what the counsel was here declaring is
that the legislature is necessarily the umpire in all disputes
between partial universes. Therefore if literature and science
should fall into a conflict, it would again be up to the legislature to assign the priority. It is not bound to recognize the
claims of either of these exclusively because, as we saw earlier,
it operates in a universe with reference to which these are
partial bodies of discourse. The legislature is the disposer of
partial universes. Accordingly when the Attorney-General
took this stand, he came the nearest of any of the participants
in the trial to clarifying the state's position, and by this we
mean to showing that for the state it was a matter of legal
dialectic.

There is little evidence to indicate that the defense understood the kind of case it was up against, though naturally this
is said in a philosophical rather than a legal sense. After the
questions of law were settled, its argument assumed the substance of a plea for the truth of evolution, which subject was
not within the scope of the indictment. We have, for example,
the statement of Mr. Hays already cited that the whole case of
the defense depended on proving that evolution is a "reasonable scientific theory." Of those who spoke for the defense,
Mr. Dudley Field Malone seems to have had the poorest conception of the nature of the contest. I must cite further from
his plea because it shows most clearly the trap from which the
defense was never able to extricate itself. On the fifth day of
the trial Mr. Malone was chosen to reply to Mr. Bryan, and in
the course of his speech he made the following revealing utterance: "Your honor, there is a difference between theological
and scientific men. Theology deals with something that is
established and revealed; it seeks to gather material which
they claim should not be changed. It is the Word of God and

that cannot be changed; it is literal, it is not to be interpreted. That is the theological mind. It deals with theology. The scientific mind is a modern thing, your honor. I am not sure Galileo was the one who brought relief to the scientific mind; because, theretofore, Aristotle and Plato had reached their conclusions and processes, by metaphysical reasoning, because they had no telescope and no microscope." The part of this passage which gives his case away is the distinction made at the end. Mr. Malone was asserting that Aristotle and Plato got no further than they did because they lacked the telescope and the microscope. To a slight extent perhaps Aristotle was what we would today call a "research scientist," but the conclusions and processes arrived at by the metaphysical reasoning of the two are dialectical, and the test of a dialectical position is logic and not ocular visibility. At the risk of making Mr. Malone a scapegoat we must say that this is an abysmal confusion of two different kinds of inquiry which the Greeks were well cognizant of. But the same confusion, if it did not produce this trial, certainly helped to draw it out to its length of eight days. It is the assumption that human laws stand in wait upon what the scientists see in their telescopes and microscopes. But harking back to Professor Adler: facts are never determinative of dialectic in the sense presumed by this counsel.

Exactly the same confusion appeared in a rhetorical plea for truth which Mr. Malone made shortly later in the same speech. Then he said: "There is never a duel with truth. The truth always wins and we are not afraid of it. The truth is no coward. The truth does not need the law. The truth does not need the forces of government. The truth does not need Mr. Bryan. The truth is imperishable, eternal and immortal and needs no human agency to support it. We are ready to tell the truth as we understand it and we do not fear all the truth that they can present as facts." It is instantly apparent that this presents truth in an ambiguous sense. Malone begins with the simplistic assumption that there is a "standard" truth, a kind of universal, objective, operative truth which it is heinous to oppose. That might be well enough if the meaning were highly generic, but before he is through this short passage he has equated truth with facts—the identical confusion which we noted in his utterance about Plato and Aristotle. Now since the truth which dialectic arrives at is not a truth of facts, this peroration either becomes irrelevant, or it lends itself to the other side, where, minus the concluding phrase, it could serve as a eulogium of dialectical truth.

Such was the dilemma by which the defense was impaled from the beginning. To some extent it appears even in the expert testimony. On the day preceding this speech by Malone, Professor Maynard Metcalf had presented testimony in court regarding the theory of evolution (this was on the fourth day of the trial; Judge Raulston did not make his ruling excluding such testimony until the sixth day) in which he made some statements which could have been of curious interest to the prosecution. They are effectually summarized in the following excerpt: "Evolution and the theories of evolution are fundamentally different things. The fact of evolution is a thing that is perfectly and absolutely clear. . . . The series of evidences is so convincing that I think it would be entirely impossible for any normal human being who was conversant with the phenomena to have even for a moment the least doubt even for the fact of evolution, but he might have tremendous doubts as to the truth of any hypothesis. . . ."

We first notice here a clear recognition of the kinds of truth distinguished by Adler, with the "fact" of evolution belonging to the first order and theories of evolution belonging to the second. The second, which is referred to by the term "hypothesis," consists of facts in an elaboration. We note furthermore that this scientist has called them fundamentally different things—so different that one is entitled to have not merely doubts but "tremendous doubts" about the second. Now let us imagine the dialecticians of the opposite side approaching him with the following. You have said, Professor Metcalf, that the fact of evolution and the various theories of evolution are two quite different things. You have also said that the theories of evolution are so debatable or questionable that you can conceive of much difference of opinion about them. Now if there is an order of knowledge above this order of theories, which order you admit to be somewhat speculative, a further order of knowledge which is philosophical or evaluative, is it not likely that there would be in this realm still more alternative positions, still more room for doubt or difference of opinion? And if all this is so, would you expect people to assent to a proposition of this order in the same way you expect them to assent to, say, the proposition that a monkey has vertebrae? And if you do make these admissions, can you any longer maintain that people of opposite views on the teaching of evolution are simply defiers of the truth? This is how the argument might have progressed had some Greek Darwin thrown Athens into an uproar; but this argument was, after all, in an American court of law.

It should now be apparent from these anlyses that the defense was never able to meet the state's case on dialectical grounds. Even if it had boldly accepted the contest on this level, it is difficult to see how it could have won, for the dialectic must probably have followed this course: First Proposition, All teaching of evolution is harmful. Counter Proposition, No teaching of evolution is harmful. Resolution, Some teaching of evolution is harmful. Now the resolution was exactly the position taken by the law, which was that some teaching of evolution (i.e., the teaching of it in state-supported schools) was an anti-social measure. Logically speaking, the proposition that "Some teaching of evolution is harmful," does not exclude the proposition that "Some teaching of evolution is not harmful," but there was the fact that the law permitted some teaching of evolution (e.g., the teaching of it in schools not supported by the public funds). In this situation there seemed nothing for the defense to do but stick by the second proposition and plead for that proposition rhetorically.

So science entered the juridical arena and argued for the value of science. In this argument the chief topic was consequence. There was Malone's statement that without the theory of evolution Burbank would not have been able to produce his results. There was Lipman's statement that without an understanding of the theory of evolution the agricultural colleges could not carry on their work. There were the statements of Judd and Nelson that large areas of education depended upon a knowledge of evolution. There was the argument brought out by Professor Mather of Harvard: "When men are offered their choice between science, with its confident and unanimous acceptance of the evolutionary principle, on the one hand, and religion, with its necessary appeal to things unseen and unprovable, on the other, they are much more likely to abandon religion than to abandon science. If such a choice is forced upon us, the churches will lose many of their best educated young people, the very ones upon whom they must depend for leadership in coming years."

We noted at the beginning of this chapter that rhetoric deals with subjects at the point where they touch upon actuality or prudential conduct. Here the defense looks at the policy of teaching evolution and points to beneficial results. The argument then becomes: these important benefits imply an important beneficial cause. This is why we can say that the pleaders for science were forced into the non-scientific role of the rhetorician.

The prosecution incidentally also had an argument from consequences, although it was never employed directly. When Bryan maintained that the philosophy of evolution might lead to the same results as the philosophy of Nietzsche had led with Loeb and Leopold, he was opening a subject which could have supplied such an argument, say in the form of a concrete instance of moral beliefs weakened by someone's having been indoctrinated with evolution. But there was really no need: as we have sought to show all along, the state had an immense strategic advantage in the fact that laws belong to the category of dialectical determinations, and it clung firmly to this advantage.

An irascible exchange which Darrow had with the judge gives an idea of the frustration which the defense felt at this stage. There had been an argument about the propriety of a cross-examination.

The Court: Colonel [Darrow], what is the purpose of cross-examination?

Mr. Darrow: The purpose of cross–examination is to be used on trial.

The Court: Well, isn't that an effort to ascertain the truth?

Mr. Darrow: No, it is an effort to show prejudice. Nothing else. Has there been any effort to ascertain the truth in this case? Why not bring in the jury and let us prove it?

The truth referred to by the judge was whether the action of Scopes fell within the definition of the law; the truth referred to by Darrow was the facts of evolution (not submitted to the jury as evidence); and "prejudice" was a crystallized opinion of the theory of evolution, expressed now as law.

If we have appeared here to assign too complete a forensic victory to the prosecution, let us return, by way of recapitulating the issues, to the relationship between positive science and dialectic. Many people, perhaps a majority in this country, have felt that the position of the State of Tennessee was absurd because they are unable to see how a logical position can be taken without reference to empirical situations. But it is just the nature of logic and dialectic to be a science without any content as it is the nature of biology or any positive science to be a science of empirical content.

We see the nature of this distinction when we realize that there is never an argument, in the true sense of the term, about facts. When facts are disputed, the argument must be suspended until the facts are settled. Not until then may it be resumed, for all true argument is about the meaning of established or admitted facts. And since this meaning is always expressed in propositions, we can say further that all argument is about the systematic import of propositions. While that remains so, the truth of the theory of evolution or of any scientific theory can never be settled in a court of law. The court could admit the facts into the record, but the process of legal determination would deal with the meaning of the facts, and it could not go beyond saying that the facts comport, or do not comport, with the meanings of other propositions. Thus its task is to determine their place in a system of discourse and if possible to effect a resolution in accordance with the movement of dialectic. It is necessary that logic in its position as ultimate arbiter preserve this indifference toward that actuality which is the touchstone of scientific fact.

It is plain that those who either expected or hoped that science would win a sweeping victory in the Tennessee courtroom were the same people who believe that science can take the place of speculative wisdom. The only consolation they had in the course of the trial was the embarrassment to which Darrow brought Bryan in questioning him about the Bible and the theory of evolution (during which Darrow did lead Bryan into some dialectical traps). But in strict consideration all of this was outside the bounds of the case because both the facts of evolution and the facts of the Bible were "items not in discourse," to borrow a phrase employed by Professor Adler. That is to say, their correctness had to be determined by scientific means of investigation, if at all; but the relationship between the law and theories of man's origin could be determined only by legal casuistry, in the non-pejorative sense of that phrase.

As we intimated at the beginning, a sufficient grasp of what the case was about would have resulted in there being no case, or in there being quite a different case. As the events turned out science received, in the popular estimation, a check in the trial but a moral victory, and this only led to more misunderstanding of the province of science in human affairs. The law of the State of Tennessee won a victory which was regarded as pyrrhic because it was generally felt to have made the law and the lawmakers look foolish. This also was a disservice to the common weal. Both of these results could have been prevented if it had been understood that science is one thing and law another. An understanding of that truth would seem to require some general dissemination throughout our educated classes of a *Summa Dialectica*. This means that the educated people of our country would have to be so trained that they could see the dialectical possibility of the opposites of the beliefs they possess. And that is a very large order for education in any age.

Chapter III

EDMUND BURKE AND THE ARGUMENT FROM CIRCUMSTANCE

W<small>E ARE</small> now in position to affirm that the rhetorical study of an argument begins with a study of the sources. But since almost any extended argument will draw upon more than one source we must look, to answer the inquiry we are now starting, at the prevailing source, or the source which is most frequently called upon in the total persuasive effort. We shall say that this predominating source gives to the argument an aspect, and our present question is, what can be inferred from the aspect of any argument or body of arguments about the philosophy of its maker? All men argue alike when they argue validly because the modes of inference are formulas, from which deviation is error. Therefore we characterize inference only as valid or invalid. But the reasoner reveals his philosophical position by the source of argument which appears most often in his major premise because the major premise tells us how he is thinking about the world. In other words, the rhetorical content of the major premise which the speaker habitually uses is the key to his primary view of existence. We are of course excluding artful choices which have in view only *ad hoc* persuasions. Putting the matter now figuratively, we may say that no man escapes being branded by the premise that he regards as most efficacious in an argument. The general importance of this is that major premises, in addition to their logical function as part of a deductive argument, are expressive of values, and a characteristic major premise characterizes the user.

To see this principle in application, let us take three of the chief sources of argument recognized by the classical rhetoricians. We may look first at the source which is *genus*. All arguments made through genus are arguments based on the nature of the thing which is said to constitute the genus. What the argument from genus then says is that "generic" classes have a nature which can be predicated of their species. Thus *man* has a nature including *mortality*, which quality can therefore be predicated of the man Socrates and the man John Smith. The underlying postulate here, that things have a nature, is of course a disputable view of the world, for it involves the acceptance of a realm of essence. Yet anyone who uses such source of argument is committed to this wider assumption. Now it follows that those who habitually argue from genus are in their personal philosophy idealists. To them the idea of genus is a reflection of existence. We are saying, accordingly, that arguments which make predominant use of genus have an aspect through this source, and that the aspect may be employed to distinguish the philosophy of the author. It will be found, to cite a concrete example, that John Henry Newman regularly argues from genus; he begins with the nature of the thing and then makes the application. The question of what a university is like is answered by applying the idea of a university. The question of what man ought to study is answered by working out a conception of the nature of man. And we shall find in a succeeding essay that Abraham Lincoln, although he has become a patron for liberals and pragmatists, was a consistent user of the argument from genus. His refusal to hedge on the principle of slavery is referable to a fixed concept of the nature of man. This, then, will serve to characterize the argument from genus.

Another important source of argument is *similitude*. Whereas those who argue from genus argue from a fixed class, those who argue from similitude invoke essential (though not exhaustive) correspondences. If one were to say, for example, that whatever has the divine attribute of reason is likely to have also the divine attribute of immortality, one would be using similitude to establish a probability. Thinkers of the analogical sort use this argument chiefly. If required to characterize the outlook it implies, we should say that it expresses belief in a oneness of the world, which causes all correspondence to have probative value. Proponents of this view tend to look toward some final, transcendental unity, and as we might expect, this type of argument is used widely by poets and religionists.[1] John Bunyan used it constantly; so did Emerson.

A third type we shall mention, the type which provides our access to Burke, is the argument from *circumstance*. The argument from circumstance is, as the name suggests, the nearest of all arguments to purest expediency. This argument merely reads the circumstances—the "facts standing around"—and accepts them as coercive, or allows them to dictate the decision. If one should say, "The city must be surrendered because the besiegers are so numerous," one would be arguing not from genus, or similitude, but from a present circumstance. The expression "In view of the situation, what else are you going to do?" constitutes a sort of proposition-form for this type of argument. Such argument savors of urgency rather than of perspicacity; and it seems to be preferred by those who are easily impressed by existing tangibles. Whereas the argument from consequence attempts a forecast of results, the argument from circumstance attempts only an estimate of current conditions or pressures. By thus making present circumstance the overbearing consideration, it keeps from sight even the nexus of cause and effect. It is the least philosophical of all the sources of argument, since theoretically it stops at the level of perception of fact.

---

1. Hosea 12:10 "I have also spoken unto the prophets, and have multiplied visions, and by the ministry of the prophets I have used similitudes."

Burke is widely respected as a conservative who was intelligent enough to provide solid philosophical foundations for his conservatism. It is perfectly true that many of his observations upon society have a conservative basis; but if one studies the kind of argument which Burke regularly employed when at grips with concrete policies, one discovers a strong addiction to the argument from circumstance. Now for reasons which will be set forth in detail later, the argument from circumstance is the argument philosophically appropriate to the liberal. Indeed, one can go much further and say that it is the argument fatal to conservatism. However much Burke eulogized tradition and fulminated against the French Revolution, he was, when judged by what we are calling aspect of argument, very far from being a conservative; and we suggest here that a man's method of argument is a truer index in his beliefs than his explicit profession of principles. Here is a means whereby he is revealed in his work. Burke's voluminous controversies give us ample opportunity to test him by this rule.

There is some point in beginning with Burke's treatment of the existing Catholic question, an issue which drew forth one of his earliest political compositions and continued to engage his attention throughout his life. As early as 1765 he had become concerned with the extraordinary legal disabilities imposed upon Catholics in Ireland, and about this time he undertook a treatise entitled *Tract on the Popery Laws*. Despite the fact that in this treatise Burke professes belief in natural law, going so far as to assert that all human laws are but declaratory, the type of argument he uses chiefly is the secular argument from circumstance. After a review of the laws and penalties, he introduces his "capital consideration."

The first and most capital consideration with regard to this, as to every object, is the extent of it. And here it is necessary to premise: this system of penalty and incapacity has for its object no small sect or obscure party, but a very numerous body of men—a body which comprehends at least two thirds of the whole nation:

it amounts to 2,800,000 souls, a number sufficient for the materials constituent of a great people.[2]

He then gave his reason for placing the circumstance first.

> This consideration of the magnitude of the object ought to attend us through the whole inquiry: if it does not always affect the reason, it is always decisive on the importance of the question. It not only makes itself a more leading point, but complicates itself with every other part of the matter, giving every error, minute in itself, a character and a significance from its application. It is therefore not to be wondered at, if we perpetually recur to it in the course of this essay.[3]

The *Tract* was planned in such a way as to continue this thought, while accompanying it with discussion of the impediment to national prosperity, and of "the impolicy of those laws, as they affect the national security." This early effort established the tenor of his thinking on the subject.

While representing Bristol in Parliament, Burke alienated a part of his constituency by supporting Sir George Savile's measure to ease the restraints upon Catholics. In the famous *Speech to the Electors of Bristol* he devoted a large portion of his time to a justification of that course, and here, it is true, he made principal use of the argument from genus ("justice") and from consequence. The argument from circumstance is not forgotten, but is tucked away at the end to persuade the "bigoted enemies to liberty." There, using again his criterion of the "magnitude of the object," he said:

> Gentlemen, it is possible you may not know that the people of that persuasion in Ireland amount to at least sixteen or seventeen hundred thousand souls. I do not at all exaggerate the number. A nation to be *persecuted!* Whilst we were masters of the sea, em-

---

2. *Works of the Right Honourable Edmund Burke* (London, 1855–64), VI, 18–19. Hereafter referred to as *Works*.
3. *Loc. cit.*

bodied with America and in alliance with half the powers of the continent, we might, perhaps, in that remote corner of Europe, afford to tyrranize with impunity. But there is a revolution in our affairs which makes it prudent for us to be just.[4]

During the last decade of his life, Burke wrote a series of letters upon the Catholic question and upon Irish affairs, in which, of course, this question figured largely. In 1792 came *A Letter to Sir Hercules Langrishe, M.P.*, upon the propriety of admitting Catholics to the elective franchise. Here we find him taking a pragmatic view of liberality toward Catholics. He reasoned as follows regarding the restoration of the franchise:

If such means can with any probability be shown, from circumstances, rather to add strength to our mixed ecclesiastical and secular constitution, than to weaken it; surely they are means infinitely to be preferred to penalties, incapacities, and proscriptions continued from generation to generation.[5]

In this instance the consideration of magnitude took a more extended form:

How much more, certainly, ought they [the disqualifying laws] to give way, when, as in our case, they affect, not here and there, in some particular point or in their consequence, but universally, collectively and directly, the fundamental franchises of a people, equal to the whole inhabitants of several respectable kingdoms and states, equal to the subjects of the kings of Sardinia or of Denmark; equal to those of the United Netherlands, and more than are to be found in all the states of Switzerland. This way of proscribing men by whole nations, as it were, from all the benefits of the constitution to which they were born, I never can believe to be politic or expedient, much less necessary for the existence of any state or church in the world.[6]

---

4. *Works*, II, 155.
5. *Works*, III, 315.
6. *Works*, III, 317.

Greatly exercised over events in France, Burke came to think of Christianity as the one force with enough cohesion to check the spread of the Revolution. Then in 1795 he wrote the *Letter to William Smith, Esq.* Here he described Christianity as "the grand prejudice . . . which holds all the other prejudices together";[7] and such prejudices, as he visualized them, were essential to the fabric of society. He told his correspondent candidly: "My whole politics, at present, center in one point; and to this the merit or demerit of every measure (with me) is referable; that is, what will most promote or depress the cause of Jacobinism."[8] In a second letter to Sir Hercules Langrishe, written in the same year, he could say: "In the Catholic Question I considered only one point. Was it at the time, and in the circumstances, a measure which tended to promote the concord of the citizens."[9]

Only once did Burke approach the question of religion through what may be properly termed an argument from definition. In the last year of his life he composed *A Letter on the Affairs of Ireland,* one passage of which considers religion not in its bearing upon some practical measure, but with reference to its essential nature.

Let every man be as pious as he pleases, and in the way that he pleases; but it is agreeable neither to piety nor to policy to give exclusively all manner of civil privileges and advantages to a *negative* religion—such is the Protestant without a certain creed; and at the same time to deny those privileges to men whom we know to agree to an iota in every one *positive* doctrine, which all of us, who profess religion authoritatively taught in England, hold ourselves, according to our faculties, bound to believe.[10]

It is not purely an argument from definition, but it contains such an argument, and so contrasts with his dominant position

---

7. *Works,* VI, 52.
8. *Loc. cit.*
9. *Works,* VI, 57.
10. *Works,* VI, 88.

on a subject which engaged much of his thought and seems to have filled him with sincere feeling.

We shall examine him now on another major subject to engage his statesmanship, the rebellion of the North American Colonies against Great Britain. By common admission today, Burke's masterpiece of forensic eloquence is the speech moving his resolutions for conciliation with that disaffected part of the Empire, delivered in the House of Commons on March 22, 1775. In admiring the felicities with which this great oration undoubtedly abounds, it is easy to overlook the fact that it is from beginning to end an argument from circumstance. It is not an argument about rights or definitions, as Burke explicitly says at two or three points; it is an argument about policy as dictated by circumstances. Its burden is a plea to conciliate the colonies because they are waxing great. No subtlety of interpretation is required to establish this truth, because we can substantially establish it in the express language of Burke himself.

To see the aspect of this argument, it is useful to begin by looking at the large alternatives which the orator enumerates for Parliament in the exigency. The first of these is to change the spirit of the Colonies by rendering it more submissive. Circumventing the theory of the relationship of ruler and ruled, Burke sets aside this alternative as impractical. He admits that an effort to bring about submission would be "radical in its principle" (*i.e.*, would have a root in principle); but he sees too many obstacles in geography, ethnology, and other circumstances to warrant the trial.

The second alternative is to prosecute the Colonists as criminal. At this point, the "magnitude of the object" again enters his equation, and he would distinguish between the indictment of a single individual and the indictment of a whole people as things different in kind. The number and vigor of the Americans constitute an embarrassing circumstance. Therefore his thought issues in the oft-quoted statement "I do not know the method of drawing up an indictment against a

whole people."[11] This was said, it should be recalled, despite
the fact that history is replete with proceedings against rebel-
lious subjects.[12] But Burke had been an agent for the colony
of New York; he had studied the geography and history of the
Colonies with his usual industry; and we may suppose him to
have had a much clearer idea than his colleagues in Parliament of their power to support a conflict.

It is understandable, by this view, that his third alternative
should be "to comply with the American spirit as necessary."
He told his fellow Commoners plainly that his proposal had
nothing to do with the legal right of taxation. "My consideration is narrow, confined, and wholly limited to the policy of
the question."[13] This policy he later characterizes as "systematic indulgence." The outcome of this disjunctive argument
is then a measure to accommodate a circumstance. The circumstance is that America is a growing country, of awesome
potentiality, whose strength, both actual and imminent, makes
it advisable for the Mother Country to overlook abstract
rights. In a peroration, the topic of abstract rights is assigned
to those "vulgar and mechanical politicians," who are "not fit
to turn a wheel in the machine" of Empire.[14]

With this conclusion in mind, it will be instructive to see
how the orator prepared the way for his proposal. The entire
first part of his discourse may be described as a depiction of
the circumstance which is to be his source of argument. After
a circumspect beginning, in which he calls attention to the
signs of rebellion and derides the notion of "paper government," he devotes a long and brilliant passage to simple characterization of the Colonies and their inhabitants. The un-

---

11. *Works*, I, 476.

12. It is interesting to compare this with his statement in *An Appeal
from the New to the Old Whigs* (*Works*, III, 77): "The number engaged
in crimes, instead of turning them into laudable acts, only augments the
quantity and intensity of the guilt."

13. *Works*, I, 479.

14. *Works*, I, 509.

avoidable effect of this passage is to impress upon his hearers
the size and resources of this portion of the Empire. First he
takes up the rapidly growing population, then the extensive
trade, then the spirit of enterprise, and finally the personal
character of the Colonists themselves. Outstanding even in
this colorful passage is his account of the New England whal-
ing industry.

Whilst we follow them among the tumbling mountains of ice,
and behold them penetrating into the deepest frozen recesses of
Hudson's Bay and Davis's Straits, whilst we are looking for them
beneath the Arctic Circle, we hear that they have pierced into the
opposite region of polar cold, that they are at the antipodes, and
engaged under the frozen Serpent of the South. Falkland Island,
which seemed too remote and romantic an object for the grasp of
national ambition, is but a stage and resting-place in the progress
of their victorious industry. Nor is the equinoctial heat more dis-
couraging to them than the accumulated winter of both the poles.
We know that whilst some of them draw the line and strike the
harpoon on the coast of Africa, others run the longitude and pursue
their gigantic game along the coast of Brazil. No sea but what is
vexed by their fisheries; no climate that is not witness to their toils.
Neither the perseverance of Holland, nor the activity of France,
nor the dexterous and firm sagacity of English enterprise ever
carried this most perilous mode of hard industry to the extent to
which it has been pushed by this recent people; a people who are
still, as it were, but in the gristle; and not yet hardened into the
bone of manhood.[15]

It is the spectacle of this enterprise which induces Burke to
"pardon something to the spirit of liberty."

The long recital is closed with an appeal which may be fitly
regarded as the *locus classicus* of the argument from circumstance. For with this impressive review of the fierce spirit of
the colonists before his audience, Burke declares: "The question is, not whether the spirit deserves praise or blame, but—

15. *Works*, I, 462.

what, in the name of God, shall we do with it?"[16] The question then is not what is right or wrong, or what accords with our idea of justice or our scheme of duty; it is, how can we meet this circumstance? "I am not determining a point of law; I am restoring tranquillity."[17] The circumstance becomes the cue of the policy. We must remind ourselves that our concern here is not to pass upon the merits of a particular controversy, but to note the term which Burke evidently considered most efficacious in moving his hearers. "Political reason," he says, elsewhere, "is a computing principle."[18] Where does political reason in this instance leave him? It leaves him inevitably in the middle, keeping the Colonies, but not as taxable parts of the Empire, allowing them to pay their own charge by voluntary grants. In Burke's characteristic view, the theoretic relationship has been altered by the medium until the thirteen (by his count fourteen) colonies of British North America are left halfway between colonial and national status. The position of the Tories meant that either the Colonies would be colonies or they would terminate their relationship with the Empire. Burke's case was that by concession to circumstance they could be retained in some form, and this would be a victory for policy. Philosophers of starker principle, like Tom Paine, held that a compromise of the Burkean type would have been unacceptable in the long run even to the Americans, and the subsequent crystallization of American nationality seems to support this view. But Burke thought he saw a way to preserve an institution by making way for a large corporeal fact.

It must be confessed that Burke's interest in the affairs of India, and more specifically in the conduct of the East India Company, is not reconcilable in quite the same way with the thesis of this chapter. Certainly there is nothing in mean motives or contracted views to explain why he should have labored over a period of fourteen years to benefit a people with

16. *Works*, I, 469.
17. *Works*, I, 480.
18. *Works*, II, 335.

whom he had no contact and from whom he could expect no
direct token of appreciation. But it must be emphasized that
the subject of this essay is methods, and even in this famous
case Burke found some opportunity to utilize his favorite
source.

In 1783, years before the impeachment of Warren Hastings,
he made a long speech in Parliament attacking Fox's East
India Bill. He was by then deeply impressed by the wrongs
done the Indians by British adventurers, yet it will be observed that his *habitus* reveals itself in the following passages.
He said of the East India Company:

I do not presume to condemn those who argue *a priori* against
the propriety of leaving such extensive political power in the hands
of a company of merchants. I know much is, and much more may
be, said against such a system. But, with my particular ideas and
sentiments, I cannot go that way to work. I feel an insuperable
reluctance in giving my hand to destroy any established institution of government, upon a theory, however plausible it may be.[19]

Then shortly he continued:

To justify us in taking the administration of their affairs out of
the hands of the East India Company, as my principles, I must see
several conditions. 1st, the object affected by the abuse must be
great and important. 2nd, the abuse affecting the great object
ought to be a great abuse. 3rd, it ought to be habitual and not acci-
dental. 4th, it ought to be utterly incurable in the body as it now
stands constituted.[20]

It is pertinent to observe that Burke's first condition here is
exactly the first condition raised with reference to the Irish
Catholics and with reference to the American Colonies. It is
further characteristic of his method that the passages cited

19. *Works*, II, 179–80.
20. *Works*, II, 180.

above are followed immediately by a description of the extent
and wealth and civilization of India, just as the plea for approaching the Colonies with reconciliation was followed by a
vivid advertisement of their extent and wealth and enterprise.
The argument is for justice, but it is conditioned upon a circumstance.

When Burke undertook the prosecution of Hastings in 1788,
these considerations seemed far from his mind. The splendid
opening charge contains arguments strictly from genus, despite the renunciation of such arguments which we see above.
He attacked the charter of the East India Company by showing that it violated the idea of a charter.[21] He affirmed the
natural rights of man, and held that they had been criminally
denied in India.[22] He scorned the notion of geographical
morality. These sound like the utterances of a man committed
to abstract right. Lord Morley has some observations on Burke
which may contain the explanation. His study of Burke's career led him to feel that "direct moral or philanthropic apostle-
ship was not his function."[23] Of his interest in India, he remarked: "It was reverence rather than sensibility, a noble and
philosophic conservatism rather than philanthropy, which
raised the storm in Burke's breast against the rapacity of English adventurers in India, and the imperial crimes of Hastings."[24] If it is true that Burke acted out of reverence rather
than out of sensibility or philanthropy, what was the reverence of? It was, likely, for storied India, for an ancient and
opulent civilization which had brought religion and the arts
to a high point of development while his ancestors were yet
"in the woods." There is just enough of deference for the established and going concern, for panoply, for that which has
prestige, to make us feel that Burke was again impressed—

21. *Works*, VII, 23.
22. *Works*, VII, 99–100.
23. John Morley, *Burke* (New York, 1879), p. 127.
24. *Ibid.*, p. 129.

with an intended consequence which was noble, of course; but it is only fair to record this component of the situation.

The noble and philosophic conservatism next translated itself into a violent opposition to the French Revolution, which was threatening to bring down a still greater structure of rights and dignities, though in this instance in the name of reform and emancipation.

The French Revolution was the touchstone of Burke. Those who have regarded his position on this event as a reversal, or a sign of fatigue and senescence, have not sufficiently analyzed his methods and his sources. Burke would have had to become a new man to take any other stand than he did on the French Revolution. It was an event perfectly suited to mark off those who argue from circumstance, for it was one of the most radical revolutions on record, and it was the work of a people fond of logical rigor and clear demonstration.

Why Burke, who had championed the Irish Catholics, the American colonists, and the Indians should have championed on this occasion the nobility and the propertied classes of Europe is easy to explain. For him Europe, with all its settlements and usages, was the circumstance; and the Revolution was the challenge to it. From first to last Burke saw the grand upheaval as a contest between inherited condition and speculative insight. The circumstance said that Europe should go on; the Revolution said that it should cease and begin anew.[24a]

24a. If further evidence of Burke's respect for circumstance were needed, one could not do better than cite his sentence from the *Reflections* depicting the "circumstance" of Bourbon France (*Works*, II, 402). "Indeed, when I consider the face of the kingdom of France; the multitude and opulence of her cities; the useful magnificence of her spacious high roads and bridges; the opportunity of her artificial canals and navigations opening the conveniences of maritime communication through a continent of so immense an extent; when I turn my eyes to the stupendous works of her ports and harbours, and to her whole naval apparatus, whether for war or trade; when I bring before my view the number of her fortifications, constructed with so bold and masterly skill, and made and maintained at so prodigious a charge, presenting an armed front and impenetrable barrier to her enemies upon every side; when I recol-

Burke's position was not selfish; it was prudential within the philosophy we have seen him to hold.

Actually his *Reflections on the Revolution in France* divides itself into two parts. The first is an attempt, made with a zeal which seems almost excessive, to prove that the British government was the product of slow accretion of precedent, that it is for that reason a beneficent and stable government, and that the British have renounced, through their choice of methods in the past, any theoretical right to change their government by revolution. The second part is a miscellany of remarks on the proceedings in France, in which many shrewd observations of human nature are mingled with eloquent appeals on behalf of the *ancien régime*.

Burke appears terrified by the thought that the ultimate sources and sanctions of government should be brought out into broad daylight for the inspection of everyone, and the first effort was to clothe the British government with a kind of concealment against this sort of inspection, which could, of course, result in the testing of that government by what might have been or might yet be. The second effort was to show that France, instead of embarking on a career of progress through her daring revolution, "had abandoned her interest, that she might prostitute her virtue." It will be observed that

---

lect how very small a part of that extensive region is without cultivation, and to what complete perfection the culture of many of the best productions of the earth have been brought in France; when I reflect on the excellence of her manufactures and fabrics, second to none but ours, and in some particulars not second; when I contemplate the grand foundations of charity, public and private; when I survey the state of all the arts that beautify and polish life; when I reckon the men she has bred for extending her fame in war, her able statesmen, the multitude of her profound lawyers and theologians, her philosophers, her critics, her historians and antiquaries, her poets and her orators, sacred and profane: I behold in all this something which awes and commands the imagination, which checks the mind on the brink of precipitate and undiscriminate censure, and which demands that we should very seriously examine, what and how great are the latent vices that could authorize us at once to level so spacious a fabric with the ground."

in both of these, a presumed well-being is the source of his argument. Therefore we have the familiar recourse to concrete situation.

Circumstances (which with some gentlemen, pass for nothing) give in reality to every political principle its distinguishing color and discriminating effect. The circumstances are what render every civil and political scheme beneficial or noxious to mankind. Abstractedly speaking, government, as well as liberty, is good; yet could I, in common sense, ten years ago, have felicitated France upon her enjoyment of a government (for she then had a government) without inquiring what the nature of the government was, or how it was administered? Can I now congratulate the same nation on its freedom?[25]

In his *Letter to a Member of the National Assembly* (1791) he said:

What a number of faults have led to this multitude of misfortunes, and almost all from this one source—that of considering certain general maxims, without attending to circumstances, to times, to places, to conjectures, and to actors! If we do not attend scrupulously to all of these, the medicine of today becomes the poison of tomorrow.[26]

This was the gist of such advice as Burke had for the French. That they should build on what they had instead of attempting to found *de novo*, that they should adapt necessary changes to existing conditions, and above all that they should not sacrifice the sources of dignity and continuity in the state—these made up a sort of gospel of precedent and gradualism which he preached to the deaf ears across the Channel. We behold him here in his characteristic political position, but forced to dig a little deeper, to give his theorems a more general application, and, it is hardly unjust to say, to make what

25. *Works*, II, 282.
26. *Works*, II, 551.

really constitutes a denial of philosophy take on some semblance of philosophy. Yet Burke was certainly never at a greater height rhetorically in defending a reigning circumstance. Let us listen to him for a moment on the virtues of old Europe.

But the age of chivalry is gone. That of sophisters, econonists, and calculators has succeeded, and the glory of Europe is extinguished forever. Never, never more shall we behold that generous loyalty to rank and sex, that proud submission, that dignified obedience, the subordination of the heart, which kept alive, even in servitude itself, the spirit of an exalted freedom. The unbought grace of life, the cheap defense of nations, the nurse of manly sentiment, is gone! It is gone, that sensibility of principle, that chastity of honour, which felt a stain like a wound, which inspired courage whilst it mitigated ferocity, which ennobled whatever it touched, and under which vice itself lost half its evil, by losing all its grossness.

This mixed system of opinion and sentiment had its origin in the ancient chivalry; and the principle, though varied in its appearance by the varying state of human affairs, subsisted and influenced through a long succession of generations, even to the time we live in. If it should ever be totally extinguished, the loss I fear will be great. It is this which has given its character to modern Europe. It is this which has distinguished it under all its forms of government, and distinguished it to its advantage, from the states of Asia, and possibly from those states which flourished in the most brilliant periods of the antique world. It was this, which, without confounding ranks, has produced a noble equality and handed it down through all the gradations of social life. It was this opinion which mitigated kings into companions, and raised private men to be fellows with kings. Without force or opposition, it subdued the fierceness of pride and power; it obliged sovereigns to submit to the soft collar of social esteem, compelled stern authority to submit to elegance, and gave a dominating vanquisher of laws to be subdued by manners.

But now all is to be changed. All the pleasing illusions which made power gentle and obedience liberal, which harmonized the different shades of life, and which, by a bland assimilation, incor-

porated into politics the sentiments which beautify and soften private society, are to be dissolved by the new conquering empire of
light and reason. All the decent drapery of life is to be rudely torn
off. All the superadded ideas, furnished from the wardrobe of a
moral imagination, which the heart owns and the imagination rati-
fies, as necessary to cover the defects of our naked, shivering nature, and to raise it to dignity in our own estimation, are to be
exposed as ridiculous, absurd, and antiquated fashions.[27]

With the writings on French affairs, Burke's argument from
circumstance came full flower.

These citations are enough to show a partiality toward
argument of this aspect. But a rehearsal of his general observations on politics and administration will show it in even
clearer light. Burke had an obsessive dislike of metaphysics
and the methods of the metaphysician. There is scarcely a
peroration or passage of appeal in his works which does not
contain a gibe, direct or indirect, at this subject. In the *Speech
On American Taxation* he said, "I do not enter into these metaphysical distinctions; I hate the very sound of them."[28] This
science he regarded as wholly incompatible with politics, yet
capable of deluding a certain type of politician with its nice-
ties and exactitudes. Whenever Burke introduced the subject
of metaphysics, he was in effect arguing from contraries; that
is to say, he was asserting that what is metaphysically true is
politically false or unfeasible. For him, metaphysical clarity
was at the opposite pole from political prudence. As he observed in the *Reflections*, "The pretended rights of these theories are all extremes; and in proportion as they are metaphysically true, they are morally and politically false."[29] In
the first letter to Sir Hercules Langrishe, he ridiculed "the
metaphysicians of our times, who are the most foolish of men,
and who, dealing in universals and essences, see no difference

---

27. *Works*, II, 348–49.
28. *Works*, I, 432.
29. *Works*, II, 335.

between more and less."[30] It will be noted that this last is a philosophical justification for his regular practice of weighing a principle by the scale of magnitude of situation. The "more and less" thus becomes determinative of the good. "Metaphysics cannot live without definition, but prudence is cautious how she defines,"[31] he said in the *Appeal from the New to the Old Whigs*. And again in the *Reflections*, "These metaphysic rights, entering into common life, like rays of light which pierce into a dense medium are by the laws of nature refracted from a straight line. Indeed, in the gross and complicated mass of human passions and concerns, the primitive rights of man undergo such a variety of refractions and reflections, that it becomes absurd to talk of them as if they continued in the simplicity of their original direction."[32] Finally, there is his clear confession, "Whenever I speak against a theory, I mean always a weak, erroneous, fallacious, unfounded theory, and one of the ways of discovering that it is a false theory is by comparing it with practice." This is the philosophical explanation of the source in circumstance of Burke's characteristic argument.

In a brilliant passage on the American character, he had observed that the Americans were in the habit of judging the pressure of a grievance by the badness of the principle rather than *vice versa*. Burke's own habit, we now see, was fairly consistently the reverse: he judged the badness of the principle by the pressure of the grievance; and hence we are compelled to suppose that he believed politics ought to be decided empirically and not dialectically. Yet a consequence of this position is that whoever says he is going to give equal consideration to circumstance and to ideals (or principles) almost inevitably finds himself following circumstances while preserving a mere decorous respect for ideals.

Burke's doctrine of precedent, which constitutes a central

---

30. *Works*, III, 317–18.
31. *Works*, III, 16.
32. *Works*, II, 334.

part of his political thought, is directly related with the above position. If one is unwilling to define political aims with reference to philosophic absolutes, one tries to find guidance in precedent. We have now seen that a principal topic of the *Reflections* is a defense of custom against insight. Burke tried with all his eloquence to show that the "manly" freedom of the English was something inherited from ancestors, like a valuable piece of property, increased or otherwise modified slightly to meet the needs of the present generation, and then reverently passed on. He did not want to know the precise origin of the title to it, nor did he want philosophical definition of it. In fact, the statement of Burke which so angered Thomas Paine—that Englishmen were ready to take up arms to prove that they had no right to change their government—however brash or paradoxical seeming, was quite in keeping with such conviction. Since he scorned that freedom which did not have the stamp of generations of approval upon it, he attempted to show that freedom too was a matter of precedent.

Yet this is an evasion rather than an answer to the real question which is lying in wait for Burke's political philosophy. It is essential to see that government either moves with something in view or it does not, and to say that people may be governed merely by following precedent begs the question. What line do the precedents mark out for us? How may we know that this particular act is in conformity with the body of precedents unless we can abstract the essence of the precedents? And if one extracts the essence of a body of precedents, does not one have a "speculative idea"? However one turns, one cannot evade the truth that there is no practice without theory, and no government without some science of government. Burke's statement that a man's situation is the preceptor of his duty cannot be taken seriously unless one can isolate the precept.

This dilemma grows out of Burke's own reluctance to speculate about the origin and ultimate end of government. "There is a sacred veil to be drawn over the beginnings of all governments," he declared in his second day's speech at the trial of Warren Hastings.[33] To the abstract doctrines of the French Revolution, he responded with a "philosophic analogy," by which governments are made to come into being with something like the indistinct remoteness of the animal organism. This political organism is a "mysterious incorporation," never wholly young or middle-aged or old, but partly each at every period, and capable, like the animal organism, of regenerating itself through renewal of tissue. It is therefore modified only through the slow forces that produce evolution. But to the question of what brings on the changes in society, Burke was never able to give an answer. He had faced the problem briefly in the *Tract on the Popery Laws*, where he wrote: "Is, then, no improvement to be brought into society? Undoubtedly, but not by compulsion—but by encouragement, but by countenance, favor, privileges, which are powerful and are lawful instruments."[34] These, however, are the passive forces which admit change, not the active ones which initiate it. The prime mover is still to seek. If such social changes are brought about by immanent evolutionary forces, they are hardly voluntary; if on the other hand they are voluntary, they must be identifiable with some point in time and with some agency of initiation. It quickly becomes obvious that if one is to talk about the beginnings of things, about the nisus of growth or of accumulation of precedents, and about final ends, one must shift from empirical to speculative ground. Burke's attachment to what was *de facto* prevented him from doing this in political theory and made him a pleader from circumstance at many crucial points in his speeches. One can scarcely do better than quote the judgment of Sir James Prior in his summation of Burke's career: "His aim therefore in our domestic policy, was to preserve all our institutions in the main as they stood for the simple reason that under them the nation had

33. *Works*, VII, 60.
34. *Works*, VI, 34.

become great, and prosperous, and happy."[35] This is but a generalized translation of the position "If it exists, there is something to be said in its favor," which we have determined as the aspect of the great orator's case.

That position is, moreover, the essential position of Whiggism as a political philosophy. It turns out to be, on examination, a position which is defined by other positions because it will not conceive ultimate goals, and it will not display on occasion a sovereign contempt for circumstances as radical parties of both right and left are capable of doing. The other parties take their bearing from some philosophy of man and society; the Whigs take their bearings from the other parties. Whatever a party of left or right proposes, they propose (or oppose) in tempered measure. Its politics is then cautionary, instinctive, trusting more to safety and to present success than to imagination and dramatic boldness of principle. It is, to make the estimate candid, a politics without vision and consequently without the capacity to survive.

"The political parties which I call great," Tocqueville wrote in *Democracy in America,* "are those which cling to principles rather than to their consequences, to general and not to special cases, to ideas and not to men."[36] Manifestly the Whig Party is contrary to this on each point. The Whigs do not argue from principles (*i.e.,* genera and definitions); they are awed not merely by consequences but also by circumstances; and as for the general and the special, we have now heard Burke testify on a dozen occasions to his disregard of the former and his veneration of the latter. There is indeed ground for saying that Burke was more Whig than the British Whigs of his own day themselves, because at the one time when the British Whig Party took a turn in the direction of radical principle, Burke found himself out of sympathy with it and, before long, was excluded from it. This occurred in

---

35. *A Life of Edmund Burke* (London, 1891), p. 523.
36. *Democracy in America* (Cambridge [Mass.], 1873), I, 226.

1791, when the electrifying influence of the French Revolution produced among the liberals of the age a strong trend toward the philosophic left. It was this trend which drew from Burke the *Appeal from the New to the Old Whigs*, with its final scornful paragraph in which he refused to take his principles "from a French die." This writing was largely taken up with a defense of his recently published *Reflections on the Revolution in France*, and it is here relevant to note how Burke defines his doctrine as a middle course. "The opinions maintained in that book," he said, "never can lead to an extreme, because their foundation is laid in an opposition to extremes."[37] "These doctrines do of themselves gravitate to a middle point, or to some point near a middle."[38] "The author of that book is supposed to have passed from extreme to extreme; but he has always actually kept himself in a medium."[39]

Actually the course of events which caused this separation was the same as that which led to the ultimate extinction of the Whig point of view in British political life. In the early twentieth century, when a world conflict involving the Empire demanded of parties a profound basis in principle, the heirs of the Whig party passed from the scene, leaving two coherent parties, one of the right and one of the left. That is part of our evidence for saying that a party which bases itself upon circumstance cannot outlast that circumstance very long; that its claim to make smaller mistakes (and to have smaller triumphs) than the extreme parties will not win it enduring allegiance; and that when the necessity arises, as it always does at some time, to look at the foundations of the commonwealth, Burke's wish will be disregarded, and only deeply founded theories will be held worthy. A party does not become great by feasting on the leavings of other parties, and Whiggism's bid for even temporary success is often rejected. A party must have its own principle of movement and must

37. *Works*, III, 109.
38. *Loc. cit.*
39. *Works*, III, 36.

not be content to serve as a brake on the movements of others. Thus there is indication that Whiggism is a recipe for political failure, but before affirming this as a conclusion, let us extend our examination further to see how other parties have fared with circumstance as the decisive argument.

The American Whig Party showed all the defects of this position in an arena where such defects were bound to be more promptly fatal. It is just to say that this party never had a set of principles. Lineal descendants of the old Federalists, the American Whigs were simply the party of opposition to that militant democracy which received its most aggressive leadership from Andrew Jackson. It was, generally speaking, the party of the "best people"; that is to say, the people who showed the greatest respect for industry and integrity, the people in whose eyes Jackson was "that wicked man and vulgar hero." Yet because it had no philosophical position, it was bound to take its position from that of the other party, as we have seen that Whiggism is doomed to do. During most of its short life it was conspicuously a party of "outs" arrayed against "ins."

It revealed the characteristic impotence in two obvious ways. First, it pinned its hopes for victory on brilliant personalities rather than on dialectically secured positions. Clay, Webster, and Calhoun, who between them represented the best statesmanship of the generation, were among its leaders, but none of them ever reached the White House. The beau ideal of the party was Clay, whose title "the Great Compromiser" seems to mark him as the archetypal Whig. Finally it discovered a politically "practical" candidate in William Henry Harrison, soldier and Indian fighter, and through a campaign of noise and irrelevancies, put him in the Presidency. But this success was short, and before long the Whigs were back battling under their native handicaps.

Second, frustrated by its series of reverses, it decided that what the patient needed was more of the disease. Whereas at the beginning it had been only relatively pragmatic in program and had preserved dignity in method, it now resolved to become completely pragmatic in program and as pragmatic as its rivals the Democrats in method. Of the latter step, the "coonskin and hard-cider" campaign on behalf of Harrison was the proof. We may cite as special evidence the advice given to Harrison's campaign manager by Nicholas Biddle of Philadelphia. "Let him [the candidate] say not a single word about his principles or his creed—let him say nothing, promise nothing. Let the use of pen and ink be wholly forbidden."[40] E. Malcolm Carroll in his *Origins of the Whig Party* has thus summed up the policy of the Whig leaders after their round with Jackson: "The most active of the Whig politicians and editors after 1836, men like Weed, Greeley, Ewing of Ohio, Thaddeus Stevens, and Richard Houghton of Boston, preferred success to a consistent position and, therefore, influenced the party to make its campaign in the form of appeal to popular emotion and, for this purpose, to copy the methods of the Democratic Party."[41] This verdict is supported by Paul Murray in his study of Whig operations in Georgia: "The compelling aim of the party was to get control of the existing machinery of government, to maintain that control, and, in some cases, to change the form of government the better to serve the dominant interest of the group."[42] Murray found that the Whigs of Georgia "naturally had a respect for the past that approached at times the unreasonable reverence of Edmund Burke for eighteenth century political institutions."[43]

But a party whose only program is an endorsement of the *status quo* is destined to go to pieces whenever the course of events brings a principle strongly to the fore. The American Union was moving toward a civil conflict in which ideological

---

40. Quoted in Marquis James, *Life of Andrew Jackson* (Indianapolis, 1937), p. 740.
41. *Origins of the Whig Party* (Durham, N. C., 1925), p. 227.
42. *The Whig Party in Georgia, 1825–1853* (Chapel Hill, 1948), p. 192.
43. *Ibid.*

differences, as deep as any that have appeared in modern revolutions, were to divide men. As always occurs in such crises, the compromisers are regarded as unreliable by both sides and are soon ejected from the scene. It now seems impossible that the Whig Party, with its political history, could have survived the fifties. But the interesting fact from the standpoint of theoretical discussion is that the Democratic Party, because it was a radically based party, was able to take over and defend certain of the defensible earlier Whig positions. Murray points out the paradoxical fact that the Democratic Party "purloined the leadership of conservative property interests in Georgia and the South."[44] It is no less paradoxical that it should have purloined the defense of the states' rights doctrine thirty years after Jackson had threatened to hang disunionists.

The paradox can be resolved only by seeing that the Whig position was one of self-stultification; and this is why a rising young political leader in Illinois of Whig affiliation left the party to lead a re-conceived Republican Party. The evidence of Lincoln's life greatly favors the supposition that he was a conservative. But he saw that conservatism to be politically effective cannot be Whiggism, that it cannot perpetually argue from circumstance. He saw that to be politically effective conservatism must have something more than a temperamental love of quietude or a relish for success. It must have some ideal objective. He found objectives in the moral idea of freedom and the political idea of union.

The political party which Abraham Lincoln carried to victory in 1860 was a party with these moral objectives. The Whigs had disintegrated from their own lack of principle, and the Republicans emerged with a program capable of rallying men to effort and sacrifice—which are in the long run psychologically more compelling than the stasis of security. But after the war and the death of the party's unique leader, all moral

44. *Op. cit.*, p. 206.

idealism speedily fell away.[45] Of the passion of revenge there was more than enough, so that some of the victor's measures look like the measures of a radical party. But the elevation of Grant to the presidency and the party's conduct during and after the Gilded Age show clearly the declining interest in reform. Before the end of the century the Republican Party had been reduced in its source of appeal to the Whig argument from circumstance (or in the case of the tariff to a wholly dishonest argument from consequences). For thirty or forty years its case came to little more than this: we are the richest nation on earth with the most widely distributed prosperity; therefore this party advocates the *status quo*. The argument, whether embodied in the phrase "the full dinner pail" or "two cars in every garage" has the same source. Murray's judgment of the Whig party in Georgia a hundred years ago: "Many facts in the history of the party might impel one to say that its members regarded the promotion of prosperity as the supreme aim of government,"[46] can be applied without the slightest change to the Republican Party of the 1920's. But when the circumstance of this *status quo* disappeared about 1930, the party's source of argument disappeared too, and no other has been found since. It became the party of frustration and hatred, and like the Whig Party earlier, it clung to personalities in the hope that they would be sufficient to carry it to victory. First there was the grass roots Middle Westerner Alf Landon; then the glamorous new convert to internationalism Wendell Willkie; then the gang-buster and Empire State governor Thomas Dewey. Finally, to make the parallel complete, there came the military hero General Dwight Eisenhower. Eisenhower can be called the William Henry Harrison of the Re-

---

45. Most of Lincoln's associates in Illinois—including David Davis, Orville H. Browning, John M. Palmer, Lyman Trumbull, Leonard Swett, and Ward Hill Lamon—who had been ardent Republicans before the war, left the party in the years following. See David Donald, *Lincoln's Herndon* (New York, 1948), p. 263.

46. *Op. cit.*, p. 203.

publican Party. He is "against" what the Democrats are doing, and he is admired by the "best" people. All this is well suited to take minds off real issues through an outpouring of national vanity and the enjoyment of sensation.

The Republican charge against the incumbent administration has been consistently the charge of "bungling," while those Republicans who have based their dissent on something more profound and clear-sighted have generally drawn the suspicion and disapproval of the party's supposedly practical leaders. Of this the outstanding proof is the defeat of the leadership of Taft. To look at the whole matter in an historical frame of reference, there has been so violent a swing toward the left that the Democrats today occupy the position once occupied by the Socialists; and the Republicans, having to take their bearings from this, now occupy the center position, which is historically reserved for liberals. Their series of defeats comes from a failure to see that there is an intellectually defensible position on the right. They persist with the argument from circumstance, which never wins any major issues, and sometimes, as we have noted, they are left without the circumstance.

I shall suggest that this story has more than an academic interest for an age which has seen parliamentary government exposed to insults, some open and vicious, some concealed and insidious. There are in existence many technological factors which themselves constitute an argument from circumstance for one-party political rule. Indeed, if the trend of circumstances were our master term, we should almost certainly have to favor the one-party efficiency system lately flourishing in Europe. The centralization of power, the technification of means of communication, the extreme peril of political divisiveness in the face of modern weapons of war, all combine to put the question, "What is the function of a party of opposition in this streamlined world anyhow?" Its proper function is to talk, but talking, unless it concerns some opposition of principles, is but the wearisome contention of "ins" and "outs." Democracy is a dialectical process, and unless society can produce a group sufficiently indifferent to success to oppose the ruling group on principle rather than according to opportunity for success, the idea of opposition becomes discredited. A party which can argue only from success has no rhetorical topic against the party presently enjoying success.

The proper aim of a political party is to persuade, and to persuade it must have a rhetoric. As far as mere methods go, there is nothing to object to in the argument from circumstance, for undeniably it has a power to move. Yet it has this power through a widely shared human weakness, which turns out on examination to be shortsightedness. This shortsightedness leads a party to positions where it has no policy, or only the policy of opposing an incumbent. When all the criteria are brought to bear, then, this is an inferior source of argument, which reflects adversely upon any habitual user and generally punishes with failure. Since, as we have seen, it is grounded in the nature of a situation rather than in the nature of things, its opposition will not be a dialectically opposed opposition, any more than was Burke's opposition to the French Revolution. And here, in substance, I would say, is the great reason why Burke should not be taken as prophet by the political conservatives. True, he has left many wonderful materials which they should assimilate. His insights into human nature are quite solid propositions to build with, and his eloquence is a lesson for all time in the effective power of energy and imagery. Yet these are the auxiliary rhetorical appeals. For the rhetorical appeal on which it will stake its life, a cause must have some primary source of argument which will not be embarrassed by abstractions or even by absolutes—the general ideas mentioned by Tocqueville. Burke was magnificent at embellishment, but of clear rational principle he had a mortal distrust. It could almost be said that he raised "muddling through" to the height of a science, though in actuality it can never be a science. In the most critical undertaking of all, the choice of one's source of argument, it would be blindness to take him as mentor. To find what Burke lacked, we now turn to the American Abraham Lincoln, who despite an imperfect education, discovered that political arguments must ultimately be based on genus or definition.

Chapter IV

ABRAHAM LINCOLN AND THE
ARGUMENT FROM DEFINITION

A LTHOUGH most readers of Lincoln sense the prevailing
aspect of his arguments, there has been no thoughtful
treatment of this interesting subject. Albert Beveridge
merely alludes to it in his observation that "In trials in cir-
cuit courts Lincoln depended but little on precedents; he
argued largely from first principles."[1] Nicolay and Hay, in
describing Lincoln's speech before the Republican Banquet
in Chicago, December 10, 1856, report as follows: "Though
these fragments of addresses give us only an imperfect reflection of the style of Mr. Lincoln's oratory during this period,
they nevertheless show its essential characteristics, a pervading clearness of analysis, and that strong tendency toward
axiomatic definition which gives so many of his sentences their
convincing force and durable value."[2] W. H. Herndon, who
had the opportunity of closest personal observation, was perhaps the most analytical of all when he wrote: "Not only were
nature, man, and principle suggestive to Mr. Lincoln; not only
had he accurate and exact perceptions, but he was causative;
his mind apparently with an automatic movement, ran back
behind facts, principles, and all things to their origin and first
cause—to the point where forces act at once as effect and

1. *Abraham Lincoln* (Boston and New York, 1928), II, 549.
2. John G. Nicolay and John Hay, *Abraham Lincoln: A History*
(New York, 1904), II, 46.

cause."[3] He observed further in connection with Lincoln's practice before the bar: "All opponents dreaded his originality, his condensation, definition, and force of expression. . . ."[4]

Our feeling that he is a father of the nation even more convincingly than Washington, and that his words are words of wisdom when compared with those of the more intellectual Jefferson and the more academic Wilson strengthen the supposition that he argued from some very fundamental source. And when we find opinion on the point harmonious, despite the wide variety of description his character has undergone, we have enough initial confirmation to go forward with the study—a study which is important not alone as showing the man in clearer light but also as showing upon what terms conservatism is possible.

It may be useful to review briefly the argument from definition. The argument from definition, in the sense we shall employ here, includes all arguments from the nature of the thing. Whether the genus is an already recognized convention, or whether it is defined at the moment by the orator, or whether it is left to be inferred from the aggregate of its species, the argument has a single postulate. The postulate is that there exist classes which are determinate and therefore predicable. In the ancient proposition of the schoolroom, "Socrates is mortal," the class of mortal beings is invoked as a predicable. Whatever is a member of the class will accordingly have the class attributes. This might seem a very easy admission to gain, but it is not so from those who believe that genera are only figments of the imagination and have no self-subsistence. Such persons hold, in the extreme application of their doctrine, that all deduction is unwarranted assumption; or that attributes cannot be transferred by imputation from genus to species. The issue here is very deep, going back to the immemorial quarrel over universals, and we shall not here

---

3. *Herndon's Lincoln* (Springfield, Ill., 1921), III, 594.
4. *Ibid.*, p. 595.

explore it further than to say that the argument from definition
or genus involves a philosophy of being, which has divided
and probably will continue to divide mankind. There are those
who seem to feel that genera are imprisoning bonds which
serve only to hold the mind in confinement. To others, such
genera appear the very organon of truth. Without going into
that question here, it seems safe to assert that those who believe in the validity of the argument from genus are idealists,
roughly, if not very philosophically, defined. The evidence
that Lincoln held such belief is overwhelming; it characterizes
his thinking from an early age; and the greatest of his utterances (excepting the Gettysburg Address, which is based
upon similitude) are chiefly arguments from definition.

In most of the questions which concerned him from the time
he was a struggling young lawyer until the time when he was
charged with the guidance of the nation, Lincoln saw opportunity to argue from the nature of man. In fact, not since the
Federalist papers of James Madison had there been in American political life such candid recourse to this term. I shall
treat his use of it under the two heads of argument from a
concept of human nature and argument from a definition of
man.

Lincoln came early to the conclusion that human nature is
a fixed and knowable thing. Many of his early judgments of
policy are based on a theory of what the human being *qua*
human being will do in a given situation. Whether he had
arrived at this concept through inductive study—for which he
had varied opportunity—or through intuition is, of course, not
the question here; our interest is in the reasoning which the
concept made possible. It appears a fact that Lincoln trusted
in a uniform predictability of human nature.

In 1838, when he was only twenty-nine years old, he was
invited to address the Young Men's Lyceum of Springfield on
the topic "The Perpetuation of Our Political Institutions." In
this instance, the young orator read the danger to perpetuation in the inherent evil of human nature. His argument was

that the importance of a nation or the sacredness of a political dogma could not withstand the hunger of men for personal distinction. Now the founders of the Union had won distinction through that very role, and so satisfied themselves. But oncoming men of the same breed would be looking for similar opportunity for distinction, and possibly would not find it in tasks of peaceful construction. It seemed to him quite possible that in the future bold natures would appear who would seek to gain distinction by pulling down what their predecessors had erected. To a man of this nature it matters little whether distinction is won "at the expense of emancipating slaves or enslaving freemen."[5] The fact remains that "Distinction will be his paramount object," and "nothing left to be done in the way of building up, he would set boldly to the task of pulling down."[6] In this way Lincoln held personal ambition to be distinctive of human nature, and he was willing to predict it of his fellow citizens, should their political institutions endure "fifty times" as long as they had.

Another excellent example of the use of this source appears in a speech which Lincoln made during the Van Buren administration. Agitation over the National Bank question was still lively, and a bill had been put forward which would have required the depositing of Federal funds in five regional subtreasuries, rather than in a National Bank, until they were needed for use. At a political discussion held in the Illinois House of Representatives, Lincoln made a long speech against the proposal in which he drew extensively from the topic of the nature of human nature. His reasoning was that if public funds are placed in the custody of subtreasurers, the duty and the personal interest of the custodians may conflict. "And who that knows anything of human nature doubts that in many instances interest will prevail over duty, and that the sub-

---

5. *The Life and Writings of Abraham Lincoln*, ed. Philip van Doren Stern (New York, 1940), p. 239. This source, hereafter referred to as *Writings*, is the most complete one-volume edition of Lincoln's works.

6. *Loc. cit.*

treasurer will prefer opulent knavery in a foreign land to honest poverty at home."[6] If on the other hand the funds were placed with a National Bank, which would have the privilege of using the funds, upon payment of interest, until they are needed, the duty and interest of the custodian would coincide. The Bank plan was preferable because we always find the best performance where duty and self-interest thus run together.[7] Here we see him basing his case again on the infallible tendency of human nature to be itself.

A few years later Lincoln was called upon to address the Washingtonian Temperance Society, which was an organization of reformed drink addicts. This speech is strikingly independent in approach, and as such is prophetic of the manner he was to adopt in wrestling with the great problems of union and slavery. Instead of following the usual line of the temperance advocate, with its tone of superiority and condemnation, he attacked all such approaches as not suited to the nature of man. He impressed upon his hearers the fact that their problem was the problem of human nature, "which is God's decree and can never be reversed." He then went on to say that people with a weakness for drink are not inferior specimens of the race but have heads and hearts that "will bear advantageous comparison with those of any other class." The appeal to drink addicts was to be addressed to men, and it could not take the form of denunciation "because it is not much in the nature of man to be driven to anything; still less to be driven about that which is exclusively his own business." When one seeks to change the conduct of a being of this nature, "per-

---

6. *Life and Works of Abraham Lincoln*, ed. Marion Mills Miller (New York, 1907), II, 41. This speech is not included in Stern's *Writings*.

7. This may impress some as an unduly cynical reading of human nature, but it will be found much closer to Lincoln's settled belief than many representations made with the object of eulogy. Herndon, for example, reports that he and Lincoln sometimes discussed the question of whether there are any unselfish human actions, and that Lincoln always maintained the negative. Cf. Herndon, *op. cit.*, III, 597.

suasion, kind, unassuming persuasion should ever be adopted." He then summed up his point: "Such is man and so must he be understood by those who would lead him, even to his own best interests."[8]

One further instance of this argument may be cited. About 1850 Lincoln compiled notes for an address to young men on the subject of the profession of law. Here again we find a refreshingly candid approach, looking without pretense at the creature man. One piece of advice which Lincoln urged upon young lawyers was that they never take their whole fee in advance. To do so would place too great a strain upon human nature, which would then lack the needful spur to industry. "When fully paid beforehand, you are more than a common mortal if you can feel the same interest in the case, as if something was still in prospect for you, as well as for your client."[9] As in the case of the subtreasury bill, Lincoln saw the yoking of duty and self-interest as a necessity of our nature.

These and other passages which could be produced indicate that he viewed human nature as a constant, by which one could determine policy without much fear of surprise. Everything peripheral Lincoln referred to this center. His arguments consequently were the most fundamental seen since a group of realists framed the American government with such visible regard for human passion and weakness. Lincoln's theory of human nature was completely unsentimental; it was the creation of one who had taken many buffetings and who, from early bitterness and later indifference, never affiliated with any religious denomination. But it furnished the means of wisdom and prophecy.

With this habit of reasoning established, Lincoln was ideally equipped to deal with the great issue of slavery. The American civil conflict of the last century, when all its superficial ex-

---

8. Stern, *Writings*, pp. 263–64.
9. *Ibid.*, p. 330.

citements have been stripped aside, appears another debate about the nature of man. Yet while other political leaders were looking to the law, to American history, and to this or that political contingency, Lincoln looked—as it was his habit already to do—to the center; that is, to the definition of man. Was the negro a man or was he not? It can be shown that his answer to this question never varied, despite willingness to recognize some temporary and perhaps even some permanent minority on the part of the African race. The answer was a clear "Yes," and he used it on many occasions during the fifties to impale his opponents.

The South was peculiarly vulnerable to this argument, for if we look at its position, not through the terms of legal and religious argument, often ingeniously worked out, but through its actual treatment of the negro, that position is seen to be equivocal. To illustrate: in the Southern case he was not a man as far as the "inalienable rights" go, and the Dred Scott decision was to class him as a chattel. Yet on the contrary the negro was very much a man when it came to such matters as understanding orders, performing work, and, as the presence of the mulatto testified, helping to procreate the human species. All of the arguments that the pro-slavery group was able to muster broke against the stubborn fact, which Lincoln persistently thrust in their way, that the negro was somehow and in some degree a man.

For our first examination of this argument, we turn to the justly celebrated speech at Peoria, October 16, 1854. Lincoln had actually begun to lose interest in politics when the passage of the highly controversial Kansas-Nebraska Bill in May, 1854, reawakened him. It was as if his moral nature had received a fresh shock from the tendencies present in this bill; and he began in that year the battle which he waged with remarkable consistency of position until he won the presidency of the Union six years later. The Speech at Peoria can be regarded as the opening gun of this campaign.

The speech itself is a rich study in logic and rhetoric, wherein one finds the now mature Lincoln showing his gift for discovering the essentials of a question. After promising the audience to confine himself to the "naked merits" of the issue and to be "no less than national in all the positions" he took, he turned at once to the topic of domestic slavery. Here arguments from the genus "man" follow one after another. Lincoln uses them to confront the Southern people with their dilemma.

Equal justice to the South, it is said, requires us to consent to the extension of slavery to new countries. That is to say, inasmuch as you do not object to my taking my hog to Nebraska, therefore I must not object to your taking your slave. Now, I admit that this is perfectly logical, if there is no difference between hogs and Negroes. But while you thus require me to deny the humanity of the Negro, I wish to ask whether you of the South, yourselves, have ever been willing to do as much?[10]

If the Southern people regard the Negro only as an animal, how do they explain their attitude toward the slave dealer?

You despise him utterly. You do not recognize him as a friend, or even as an honest man. Your children must not play with his; they may rollick freely with the little Negroes, but not with the slave dealer's children. If you are obliged to deal with him, you try to get through the job without so much as touching him. It is common with you to join hands with men you meet, but with the slave dealer you avoid the ceremony—instinctively shrinking from the snaky contact. If he grows rich and retires from business, you still remember him, and still keep up the ban of non-intercourse upon him and his family. Now why is this? You do not so treat the man who deals in corn, cotton, or tobacco?[11]

Moreover, if the Negro is merely property, and is incapable of any sort of classification, what category is there to accommodate the free Negroes?

---

10. Stern, *Writings*, pp. 359–60.
11. *Ibid.*, pp. 360–61.

And yet again. There are in the United States and Territories, including the District of Columbia, 433,643 free blacks. At five hundred dollars per head, they are worth over two hundred millions of dollars. How comes this vast amount of property to be running about without owners? We do not see free horses or free cattle running at large. How is this? All these free blacks are the descendants of slaves, or have been slaves themselves; and they would be slaves now but for something which has operated on their white owners, inducing them at vast pecuniary sacrifice to liberate them. What is that something? Is there any mistaking it? In all these cases it is your sense of justice and human sympathy continually telling you that the poor Negro has some natural right to himself—that those who deny it and make mere merchandise of him deserve kickings, contempt, and death.[12]

The argument is clinched with a passage which puts the Negro's case in the most explicit terms one can well conceive of. "Man" and "self-government," Lincoln argues, cannot be defined without respect to one another.

The doctrine of self-government is right—absolutely and eternally right—but it has no just application as here attempted. Or perhaps I should rather say that whether it has such application depends upon whether a Negro is not or is a man. If he is not a man, in that case he who is a man may as a matter of self-government do just what he pleases with him.

But if the Negro is a man, is it not to that extent a total destruction of self-government to say that he too shall not govern himself? When the white man governs himself, that is self-government; but when he governs himself and also governs another man, that is more than self-government—that is despotism. If the Negro is a man, why then my ancient faith teaches me that "all men are created equal," and that there can be no moral right in connection with one man's making a slave of another.[13]

---

12. Stern, *Writings*, p. 361.
13. *Ibid.*, p. 362.

Lincoln knew the type of argument he had to oppose, and he correctly gauged its force. It was the argument from circumstance, which he treated as such argument requires to be treated. "Let us turn slavery from its claims of 'moral right' back upon its existing legal rights and its argument of 'necessity.' "[14] He did not deny the "necessity"; he regarded it as something that could be taken care of in course of time.

After the formation of the Republican Party, he often utilized his source in definition to point out the salient difference between Republicans and Democrats. The Democrats were playing up circumstance (the "necessity" alluded to in the above quotation) and to consequence (the saving of the Union through the placating of all sections) while the Republicans stood, at first a little forlornly, upon principle. As he put it during a speech at Springfield in 1857:

> The Republicans inculcate, with whatever of ability they can, that the Negro is a man, that his bondage is cruelly wrong, and that the field of his oppression ought not to be enlarged. The Democrats deny his manhood; deny, or dwarf to insignificance, the wrong of his bondage; so far as possible crush all sympathy for him, and cultivate and excite hatred and disgust against him; compliment themselves as Union-savers for doing so; and call the indefinite outspreading of his bondage "a sacred right of self-government."[15]

In the long contest with Douglas and the party of "popular sovereignty," Lincoln's principal charge was that his opponents, by straddling issues and through deviousness, were breaking down the essential definition of man. Repeatedly he referred to "this gradual and steady debauching of public opinion." He made this charge because those who advocated local option in the matter of slavery were working unremittingly to change the Negro "from the rank of a man to that of a brute." "They are taking him down," he declared, "and

---

14. Stern, *Writings,* p. 375.
15. *Ibid.,* p. 427.

placing him, when spoken of, among reptiles and crocodiles, as Judge Douglas himself expresses it.

"Is not this change wrought in your minds a very important change? Public opinion in this country is everything. In a nation like ours this popular sovereignty and squatter sovereignty have already wrought a change in the public mind to the extent I have already stated. There is no man in this crowd who can contradict it.

"Now, if you are opposed to slavery honestly, I ask you to note that fact, and the like of which is to follow, to be plastered on, layer after layer, until very soon you are prepared to deal with the Negro everywhere as with a brute."[16]

We feel that the morality of intellectual integrity lay behind such resistance to the breaking down of genera. Lincoln realized that the price of honesty, as well as of success in the long run, is to stay out of the excluded middle.

In sum, we see that Lincoln could never be dislodged from his position that there is one genus of human beings; and early in his career as lawyer he had learned that it is better to base an argument upon one incontrovertible point than to try to make an impressive case through a whole array of points. Through the years he clung tenaciously to this concept of genus, from which he could draw the proposition that what is fundamentally true of the family will be true also of the branches of the family.[17] Therefore since the Declaration of Independence had interdicted slavery for man, slavery was interdicted for the negro in principle. Here is a good place to point out that whereas for Burke circumstance was often a deciding factor, for Lincoln it was never more than a retarding factor. He marked the right to equality affirmed by the signers

---

16. Stern, *Writings*, pp. 549-50.

17. Cf. the remark in "Notes for Speeches" (*Ibid.*, pp. 497-98): "Suppose it is true that the Negro is inferior to the white in the gifts of nature; is it not the exact reverse of justice that the white should for that reason take from the Negro any of the little which he has had given to him?"

of the Declaration of Independence: "They meant simply to declare the right, so that enforcement of it might follow as fast as circumstances would permit."[18] And he recognized the stubborn fact of the institution of American slavery. But he did not argue any degree of rightness from the fact. The strategy of his whole anti-slavery campaign was that slavery should be restricted to the states in which it then existed and in this way "put in course of ultimate extinction"—a phrase which he found expressive enough to use on several occasions.

There is quite possibly concealed here another argument from definition, expressible in the proposition that which cannot grow must perish. To fix limits for an institution with the understanding that it shall never exceed these is in effect to pass sentence of death. The slavery party seems to have apprehended early that if slavery could not wax, it would wane, and hence their support of the Mexican War and the Kansas-Nebraska Bill. Lincoln's inflexible defense of the terms of the old Northwest Ordinance served notice that he represented the true opposition. In this way his definitive stand drew clear lines for the approaching conflict.

To gain now a clearer view of Lincoln's mastery of this rhetoric, it will be useful to see how he used various arguments from definition within the scope of a single speech, and for this purpose we may choose the First Inaugural Address, surely from the standpoint of topical organization one of the most notable American state papers. The long political contest, in which he had displayed acumen along with tenacity, had ended in victory, and this was the juncture at which he had to lay down his policy for the American Union. For some men it would have been an occasion for description mainly; but Lincoln seems to have taken the advice he had given many years before to the Young Men's Lyceum of Springfield: "Passion has helped us but can do so no more. . . . Reason, cold, calculating, unimpassioned reason—must furnish all the mate-

---

18. Stern, *Writings,* p. 422.

rials for our future support and defense. . . ."[19] Without being
cold, the speech is severely logical, and much of the tone is
contributed by the type of argument preferred.

Of the fourteen distinguishable arguments in this address,
eight are arguments from definition or genus. Of the six re-
maining, two are from consequences, two from circumstances,
one from contraries, and one from similitude. The proportion
tells its own story. Now let us see how the eight are employed:

1. *Argument from the nature of all government.* All governments have a fundamental duty of self-preservation. "Perpetuity is implied, if not expressed, in the fundamental law of all
national governments."[20] This means of course that whatever
is recognized as a government has the obligation to defend
itself from without and from within, and whatever menaces
the government must be treated as a hostile force. This argument was offered to meet the contention of the secessionists
that the Constitution nowhere authorized the Federal government to take forcible measures against the withdrawing
states. Here Lincoln fell back upon the broader genus "all
government."

2. *Argument from the nature of contract.* Here Lincoln met
the argument that the association of the states is "in the nature
of a contract merely." His answer was that the rescinding of a
contract requires the assent of all parties to it. When one party
alone ceases to observe it, the contract is merely violated, and
violation affects the material interests of all parties. By this
interpretation of the law of contract, the Southern states could
not leave the Union without a general consent.

3. *Argument from the nature of the American Union.* Here
Lincoln began with the proposition that the American Union
is older than the Constitution. Now since the Constitution was
formed "to make a more perfect union," it must have had in
view the "vital element of perpetuity," since the omission of

19. Stern, *Writings*, p. 241.
20. *Ibid.*, p. 649.

this element would have left a less perfect union than before. The intent of the Constitution was that "no State upon its own mere motion can lawfully get out of the Union." Therefore the American Union, as an instrument of government, had in its legal nature protection against this kind of disintegration.

4. *Argument from the nature of the chief magistrate's office.* Having thus defined the Union, Lincoln next looked at the duties which its nature imposed upon the chief magistrate. He defined it as "simple duty" on the chief magistrate's part to see that the laws of this unbroken union "be faithfully executed in all the states." Obviously the argument was to justify active measures in defense of the Union. As Lincoln conceived the definition, it was not the duty of the chief magistrate to preside over the disintegration of the Union, but to carry on the executive office just as if no possibility of disintegration threatened.

Thus far, it will be observed, the speech is a series of deductions, each one deriving from the preceding definition.

5. *Argument from the nature of majority rule.* This argument, with its fine axiomatic statements, was used by Lincoln to indicate how the government should proceed in cases not expressly envisaged by the Constitution. Popular government demands acquiescence by minorities in all such cases. "If the minority will not acquiesce, the majority must, or the government will cease. There is no other alternative; for continuing the government is acquiescence on one side or the other.

"If a minority in such case will secede rather than acquiesce, they make a precedent which in turn will divide and ruin them; for a minority of their own will secede from them whenever a majority refuses to be controlled by such a minority."[21] The difficulty of the Confederacy with states' rights within its own house was to attest to the soundness of this argument.

6. *Argument from the nature of the sovereignty of the people.* Here Lincoln conceded the right of the whole people to

---

21. Stern, *Writings*, pp. 652–53.

change its government by constitutional reform or by revolutionary action. But he saw this right vested in the people as a whole, and he insisted that any change be carried out by the modes prescribed. The institutions of the country were finally the creations of the sovereign will of the people. But until a will on this issue was properly expressed, the government had a commission to endure as before.

7. *Second argument from the nature of the office of chief magistrate.* This argument followed the preceding because Lincoln had to make it clear that whereas the people, as the source of sovereign power, had the right to alter or abolish their government, the chief magistrate, as an elected servant, had no such right. He was chosen to conduct the government then in existence. "His duty is to administer the present government as it came into his hands, and to transmit it, unimpaired by him, to his successor."[22]

8. *Second argument from the nature of the sovereignty of the people.* In this Lincoln reminds his audience that the American government does not give its officials much power to do mischief, and that it provides a return of power to the people at short intervals. In effect, the argument defines the American type of government and a tyranny as incompatible from the fact that the governors are up for review by the people at regular periods.

It can hardly be overlooked that this concentration upon definition produces a strongly legalistic speech, if we may conceive law as a process of defining actions. Every important policy of which explanation is made is referred to some widely accepted American political theory. It has been said that Lincoln's advantage over his opponent Jefferson Davis lay in a flexible-minded pragmatism capable of dealing with issues on their own terms, unhampered by metaphysical abstractions. There may be an element of truth in this if reference is made to the more confined and superficial matters—to pro-

---

22. Stern, *Writings*, p. 656.

cedural and administrative detail. But one would go far to find a speech more respectful toward the established principles of American government—to defined and agreed upon things— than the First Inaugural Address.

Although no other speech by Lincoln exhibits so high a proportion of arguments from definition, the First Message to Congress (July 4, 1861) makes a noteworthy use of this source. The withdrawal of still other states from the Union, the Confederate capture of Fort Sumter, and ensuing military events compelled Lincoln to develop more fully his anti-secessionist doctrine. This he did in a passage remarkable for its treatment of the age-old problem of freedom and authority. What had to be made determinate, as he saw it, was the nature of free government.

And this issue embraces more than the fate of these United States. It presents to the whole family of man the question of whether a constitutional republic or democracy—a government of the people by the same people—can or cannot maintain its territorial integrity against its own domestic foes. It presents the question whether discontented individuals, too few in numbers to control administration according to organic law in any case, can always, upon the pretenses made in this case, or on any other pretenses, or arbitrarily without any pretense, break up their government, and thus practically put an end to free government upon the earth. It forces us to ask: "Is there, in all republics, this inherent and fatal weakness?" "Must a government, of necessity, be too strong for the liberties of its own people, or too weak to maintain its own existence?"[23]

Then looking at the doctrine of secession as a question of the whole and its parts, he went on to say:

This relative matter of national power and State rights, as a principle, is no other than the principle of generality and locality. Whatever concerns the whole should be confined to the whole—to

---

23. Stern, *Writings*, pp. 667–68.

the General Government; while whatever concerns only the State should be left exclusively to the State. This is all there is of original principle about it. Whether the National Constitution in defining boundaries between the two has applied the principle with exact accuracy is not to be questioned. We are all bound by that defining without question.[24]

One further argument, occurring in a later speech, deserves special attention because of the clear way in which it reveals Lincoln's method. When he delivered his Second Annual Message to Congress on December 1, 1862, he devoted himself primarily to the subject of compensated emancipation of the slaves. This was a critical moment of the war for the people of the border states, who were not fully committed either way, and who were sensitive on the subject of slavery. Lincoln hoped to gain the great political and military advantage of their adherence. The way in which he approaches the subject should be of the highest interest to students of rhetoric, for the opening part of the speech is virtually a copybook exercise in definition. There he faces the question of what constitutes a nation. "A nation may be said to consist of its territory, its people, and its laws." Here we see in scholarly order the genus particularized by the differentiae. Next he enters into a critical discussion of the differentiae. The notion may strike us as curious, but Lincoln proceeds to cite the territory as the enduring part. "The territory is the only part which is of a certain durability. 'One generation passeth away and another cometh, but the earth abideth forever.' It is of the first importance to duly consider and estimate this ever-enduring part."[25] Now, Lincoln goes on to say, our present strife arises "not from our permanent part, not from the land we inhabit, not from our national homestead." It is rather the case that "Our strife pertains to ourselves—to the passing generations of men; and it can without convulsion be hushed forever with the passing of

24. Stern, *Writings*, p. 671.
25. *Ibid.*, p. 736.

one generation."[26] The present generation will soon disappear, and our laws can be modified by our will. Therefore he offers a plan whereby all owners will be indemnified and all slaves will be free by the year 1900.

Seen in another way, what Lincoln here does is define "nation" and then divide the differentiae into the permanent and the transitory; finally he accommodates his measure both to the permanent part (a territory to be wholly free after 1900) and the transitory part (present men and institutions, which are to be "paid off").

It is the utterance of an American political leader; yet it is veritably Scholastic in its method and in the clearness of its lines of reasoning. It is, at the same time, a fine illustration of pressing toward the ideal goal while respecting, but not being deflected by, circumstances.

It seems pertinent to say after the foregoing that one consequence of Lincoln's love of definition was a war-time policy toward slavery which looked to some like temporizing. We have encountered in an earlier speech his view that the Negro could not be classified merely as property. Yet it must be remembered that in the eyes of the law Negro slaves were property; and Lincoln was, after all, a lawyer. Morally he believed them not to be property, but legally they were property; and the necessity of walking a line between the moral imperative and the law will explain some of his actions which seem not to agree with the popular conception of the Great Emancipator. The first serious clash came in the late summer of 1861, when General Fremont, operating in Missouri, issued a proclamation freeing all slaves there belonging to citizens in rebellion against the United States. Lincoln first rebuked General Fremont and then countermanded his order. To O. H. Browning, of Quincy, Illinois, who had written him in support of Fremont's action, he responded as follows:

---

26. Stern, *Writings*, p. 737.

You speak of it as the only means of saving the government. On the contrary, it is itself the surrender of the government. Can it be pretended that it is any longer the Government of the United States—any government of constitution and laws—wherein a general or a president may make permanent rules of property by proclamation?[27]

This was the doctrine of the legal aspect of slavery which was to be amplified in the Second Annual Message to Congress:

Doubtless some of those who are to pay, and not to receive, will object. Yet the measure is both just and economical. In a certain sense the liberation of the slaves is the destruction of property— property acquired by descent or by purchase, the same as any other property. . . . If, then, for a common object this property is to be sacrificed, is it not just that it be done at a common charge?[28]

It is a truism that as a war progresses, the basis of the war changes, and our civil conflict was no exception. It appears to have become increasingly clear to Lincoln that slavery was not only the fomenting cause but also the chief factor of support of the secessionist movement, and finally he came to the conclusion that the "destruction" of this form of property was an indispensable military proceeding. Even here though—and contrary to the general knowledge of Americans today—definitions were carefully made. The final document was not a proclamation to emancipate slaves, but a proclamation to confiscate the property of citizens in rebellion "as a fit and necessary measure for suppressing said rebellion." Its terms did not emancipate all slaves, and as a matter of fact slavery was legal in the District of Columbia until some time after Lincoln's death.

In view of Lincoln's frequent reliance upon the argument

---

27. Stern, *Writings*, p. 682.
28. *Ibid.*, p. 740.

from definition, it becomes a matter of interest to inquire whether he appears to have realized that many of his problems were problems of definition. One can of course employ a type of argument without being aware of much more than its *ad hoc* success, but we should expect a reflective mind like Lincoln's to ponder at times the abstract nature of his method. Furthermore, the extraordinary accuracy with which he used words is evidence pointing in the same direction. Sensitivity on the score of definitions is tantamount to sensitivity on the score of names, and we find the following in the First Message to Congress:

> It might seem, at first thought, to be of little difference whether the present movement at the South be called "secession" or "rebellion." The movers, however, well understand the difference. At the beginning they knew they could never raise their reason to any respectable magnitude by any name which implies violation of law.[29]

Lincoln must at times have viewed his whole career as a battle against the "miners and sappers" of those names which expressed the national ideals. His chief charge against Douglas and the equivocal upholders of "squatter sovereignty" was that they were trying to circumvent definitions, and during the war period he had to meet the same sort of attempts. Lincoln's most explicit statement by far on the problem appears in a short talk made at one of the "Sanitary Fairs" it was his practice to attend. Speaking this time at Baltimore in the spring of 1864, he gave one of those timeless little lessons which have made such an impression on men's minds.

> The world has never had a good definition of the word liberty, and the American people, just now, are much in want of one. We all declare for liberty; but in using the same word we do not all mean the same thing. With some the word liberty may mean for

---

29. Stern, *Writings*, p. 669.

each man to do as he pleases, with himself, and with the product
of his labor; while with others the same word may mean for some
men to do as they please with other men, and the product of other
men's labor. Here are two, not only different, but incompatible
things, called by the same name, liberty. And it follows that each
of the things is, by the respective parties, called by two different
and incompatible names—liberty and tyranny.

The shepherd drives the wolf from the sheep's throat, for which
the sheep thanks the shepherd as his liberator, while the wolf
denounces him for the same act, as the destroyer of liberty, especially as the sheep was a black one. Plainly, the sheep and the wolf
are not agreed upon a definition of the word liberty; and precisely
the same difference prevails today among us human creatures, even
in the North, and all professing to love liberty.[30]

So the difficulty appeared in his time, and it should hardly be
necessary to point out that no period of modern history has
been more in need of this little homily on the subject of definition than the first half of the twentieth century.

The relationship between words and essences did then
occur to Lincoln as a problem, and we can show how he was
influenced in one highly important particular by his attention
to this relationship.

Fairly early in his struggle against Douglas and others
whom he conceived to be the foes of the Union, Lincoln became convinced that the perdurability of laws and other institutions is bound up with the acceptance of the principle of
contradiction. Or, if that seems an unduly abstract way of
putting the matter, let us say that he came to repudiate, as
firmly as anyone in practical politics may do, those people who
try by relativistic interpretations and other sophistries to
evade the force of some basic principles. The heart of Lincoln's statesmanship, indeed, lay in his perception that on
some matters one has to say "Yes" or "No," that one has to
accept an alternative to the total exclusion of the other, and

---

30. Stern, *Writings*, pp. 810–11.

that any weakness in being thus bold is a betrayal. Let us examine some of the stages by which this conviction grew upon him.

It seems not generally appreciated that this position comprises the essence of the celebrated "House Divided" speech, delivered before the Republican State Convention at Springfield, June 16, 1858. There he said: " 'A house divided against itself cannot stand.' I believe this government cannot endure permanently half slave and half free. I do not expect the Union to be dissolved—I do not expect the house to fall—but I do expect it will cease to be divided. It will become all one thing or all the other."[31] How manifest it is that Lincoln's position was not one of "tolerance," as that word is vulgarly understood today. It was a definite insistence upon right, with no regard for latitude and longitude in moral questions. For Lincoln such questions could neither be relativistically decided nor held in abeyance. There was no middle ground. In the light of American political tradition the stand is curiously absolute, but it is there—and it is genuinely expressive of Lincoln's matured view.

Douglas had made the fatal mistake of looking for a position in the excluded middle. He had been trying to get slavery admitted into the territories by feigning that the institution was morally indifferent. His platform declaration had been that he did not care "whether it is voted up or voted down" in the territories. That statement made a fine opening for Lincoln, which he used as follows in his reply at Alton:

Any man can say that who does not see anything wrong in slavery, but no man can logically say it who does see a wrong in it; because no man can logically say he don't care whether a wrong is voted up or down. He may say he don't care whether an indifferent thing is voted up or down, but he must logically have a choice between a right thing and a wrong thing. He contends that whatever community wants slaves has a right to have them. So they

31. Stern, *Writings*, p. 429.

have if it is not a wrong. But if it is a wrong, he cannot say people have a right to do a wrong.[32]

In a speech at Cincinnati the following year, he used a figure from the Bible to express his opposition to compromise. "The good old maxims of the Bible are applicable, and truly applicable, to human affairs, and in this, as in other things, we may say here that he who is not for us is against us; he who gathereth not with us scattereth."[33] In the Address at Cooper Union Institute, February 27, 1860, Lincoln took long enough to describe the methodology of this dodge by Douglas and his supporters. It was, as we have indicated, an attempt to squeeze into the excluded middle. "Let us be diverted by none of those sophistical contrivances wherewith we are so industriously plied and belabored—contrivances such as groping for some middle ground between the right and the wrong: vain as the search for a man who should be neither a living man nor a dead man; such as a policy of 'don't care' on a question about which all true men do care...."[34] Finally, and most eloquently of all, there is the brief passage from his "Meditation on the Divine Will," composed sometime in 1862. "The will of God prevails. In great contests each party claims to act in accordance with the will of God. Both may be, and one must be, wrong. God cannot be for and against the same thing at the same time."[35] God too is a rational being and will not be found embracing both sides of a contradictory. Where mutual negation exists, God must be found on one side, and Lincoln hopes, though he does not here claim, that God is in the Union's corner of this square of opposition.

The fact that Lincoln's thought became increasingly logical under the pressure of events is proof of great depths in the man.

32. Stern, *Writings*, pp. 529–30.
33. *Ibid.*, p. 558.
34. *Ibid.*, p. 591.
35. *Ibid.*, p. 728.

Now as we take a general view of Lincoln's habit of defining in its relation to his political thought, we see that it gave him one quality in which he is unrivalled by any other American leader—the quality of perspective. The connection of the two is a necessary one. To define is to assume perspective; that is the method of definition. Since nothing can be defined until it is placed in a category and distinguished from its near relatives, it is obvious that definition involves the taking of a general view. Definition must see the thing in relation to other things, as that relation is expressible through substance, magnitude, kind, cause, effect, and other particularities. It is merely different expression to say that this is a view which transcends: perspective, detachment, and capacity to transcend are all requisites of him who would define, and we know that Lincoln evidenced these qualities quite early in life,[36] and that he employed them with consummate success when the future of the nation depended on his judgment.

Let us remember that Lincoln was a leader in the most bitter partisan trial in our history; yet within short decades after his death he had achieved sanctuary. His name is now immune against partisan rancor, and he has long ceased to be a mere sectional hero. The lesson of these facts is that greatness is found out and appreciated just as littleness is found out and scorned, and Lincoln proved his greatness through his habit of transcending and defining his objects. The American scene of his time invites the colloquial adjective "messy"—with human slavery dividing men geographically and spiritually, with a fluid frontier, and with the problems of labor and capital and of immigration already beginning to exert their pressures—but Lincoln looked at these things in perspective and refused to look at them in any other way.

For an early example of this characteristic vision of his, we may go back to the speech delivered before the Young Men's

---

36. The homeric fits of abstraction, which almost every contemporary reports, are highly suggestive of the mind which dwells with essences.

Lyceum in 1838. The opening is significant. "In the great journal of things happening under the sun, we the American people, find our account running under date of the nineteenth century of the Christian era. We find ourselves in the peaceful possession of the fairest portion of the earth as regards extent of territory, fertility of soil, and salubrity of climate."[37] So Lincoln takes as his point of perspective all time, of which the Christian era is but a portion; and the entire earth, of which the United States can be viewed as a specially favored part. This habit of viewing things from an Olympian height never left him. We might cite also the opening of the Speech at Peoria, and that of the Speech at the Cooper Union Institute; but let us pass on twenty-five years and re-read the first sentence of the Gettysburg Address. "Fourscore and seven years ago our fathers brought forth on this continent a new nation, conceived in liberty and dedicated to the proposition that all men are created equal." Again tremendous perspective, suggesting almost that Lincoln was looking at the little act from some ultimate point in space and time. "Fourscore and seven years ago" carries the listener back to the beginning of the nation. "This continent" again takes the whole world into purview. "Our fathers" is an auxiliary suggestion of the continuum of time. The phrase following defines American political philosophy in the most general terms possible. The entire opening sentence, with its sustained detachment, sounds like an account of the action to be rendered at Judgment Day. It is not Abe Lincoln who is speaking the utterance, but the voice of mankind, as it were, to whom the American Civil War is but the passing vexation of a generation. And as for the "brave men, living and dead, who struggled here," it takes two to make a struggle, and is there anything to indicate that the men in gray are excluded? There is nothing explicit, and therefore we may say that Lincoln looked as far ahead as he looked behind in commemorating the event of Gettysburg.

---

37. Stern, *Writings*, p. 231.

This habit of perspective led Lincoln at times to take an extraordinarily objective view of his own actions—more frequently perhaps as he neared the end of his career. It was as if he projected a view in which history was the duration, the world the stage, and himself a transitory actor upon it. Of all his utterances the Second Inaugural is in this way the most objective and remote. Its tone even seems that of an actor about to quit the stage. His self-effacement goes to the extent of impersonal constructions, so that in places Lincoln appears to be talking about another person. "At this second appearing to take the oath of the Presidential office, there is less occasion for an extended address than there was at the first." "At this second appearing"! Is there any way of gathering, except from our knowledge of the total situation, who is thus appearing? Then after a generalized review of the military situation, he declares: "With high hope for the future, no prediction in regard to it is ventured." Why "is ventured" rather than "I venture"? Lincoln had taught himself to view the war as one of God's processes worked out through human agents, and the impersonality of tone of this last and most deeply meditative address may arise from that habit. Only once, in the modest qualifying phrase "I trust," does the pronoun "I" appear; and the final classic paragraph is spoken in the name of "us." There have been few men whose processes of mind so well deserve the epithet *sub specie aeternitatis* as Lincoln's.

It goes without further demonstration that Lincoln transcended the passions of the war. How easy it is for a leader whose political and personal prestige are at stake to be carried along with the tide of hatred of a people at war, we have, unhappily, seen many times. No other victor in a civil conflict has conducted himself with more humanity, and this not in some fine gesture after victory was secured—although there was that too—but during the struggle, while the issue was still in doubt and maximum strain was placed upon the feelings. Without losing sight of his ultimate goal, he treated everyone with personal kindness, including people who went out of their way in attempts to wound him. And probably it was his habit of looking at things through objective definitions which kept him from confusing being logically right with being personally right. In the "Meditation on the Divine Will" he wrote, "In the present civil war it is quite possible that God's purpose is something different from the purpose of either party. . . ."[38] That could be written only by one who has attained the highest level of self-discipline. It explains too why he should write, in his letter to Cuthbert Bullitt: "I shall do nothing in malice. What I deal with is too vast for malicious dealing."[39] Lastly, there is the extraordinary confession of common guilt in the Second Inaugural Address, which, if it had been honored by the government he led, would have constituted a step without precedent in history in the achievement of reconciliation after war. It is supposable, Lincoln said, that God has given "to both North and South this terrible war." Hardly seventy-five years later we were to see nations falling into the ancient habit of claiming exclusive right in their quarrels and even of demanding unconditional surrender. As late as February, 1865, Lincoln stood ready to negotiate, and his offer, far from requiring "unconditional surrender," required but one condition—return of the seceded states to the Union.

There is, when we reflect upon the matter, a certain morality in clarity of thought, and the man who had learned to define with Euclid and who had kept his opponents in argument out of the excluded middle, could not be pushed into a settlement which satisfied only passion. The settlement had to be objectively right. Between his world view and his mode of argument and his response to great occasions there is a relationship so close that to speak of any one apart is to leave the exposition incomplete.

With the full career in view, there seems no reason to differ with Herndon's judgment that Lincoln displayed a high order

38. Stern, *Writings*, p. 728.
39. *Ibid.*, p. 710.

of "conservative statesmanship."[40] It is true that Lincoln has been placed in almost every position, from right to left, on the political arc. Our most radical parties have put forward programs in his name; and Professor J. G. Randall has written an unconvincing book on "Lincoln the Liberal Statesman." Such variety of estimate underlines the necessity of looking for some more satisfactory criterion by which to place the man politically. It will not do to look simply at the specific measures he has supported. If these were the standard, George Washington would have to be regarded as a great progressive; Imperial Germany would have to be regarded as liberal, or even as radical, by the token of its social reforms. It seems right to assume that a much surer index to a man's political philosophy is his characteristic way of thinking, inevitably expressed in the type of argument he prefers. In reality, the type of argument a man chooses gives us the profoundest look we get at his principle of integration. By this method Burke, who was partial to the argument from circumstance, must be described as a liberal, whose blast against the French Revolution was, even in his own words, an attack from center against an extreme. Those who argue from consequence tend to go all out for action; they are the "radicals." Those who prefer the argument from definition, as Lincoln did, are conservatives in the legitimate sense of the word. It is no accident that Lincoln became the founder of the greatest American conservative party, even if that party was debauched soon after his career ended. He did so because his method was that of the conservative.

The true conservative is one who sees the universe as a paradigm of essences, of which the phenomenology of the world is a sort of continuing approximation. Or, to put this in another way, he sees it as a set of definitions which are struggling to get themselves defined in the real world. As Lincoln remarked of the Framers of the Declaration of Independence: "They

----

40. *Op. cit.*, III, 610.

meant to set up a standard maxim for free society, which should be familiar to all, and revered by all; constantly looked to, constantly labored for, and even though never perfectly attained, constantly approximated, and thereby constantly spreading and deepening its influence and augmenting the happiness and value of life to all people of all colors everywhere."[41] This paradigm acts both as an inspiration to action and as a constraint upon over-action, since there is always a possibility of going beyond the schemata into an excess. Lincoln opposed both slavery and the Abolitionists (the Abolitionists constituted a kind of "action" party); yet he was not a middle-of-the-roader. Indeed, for one who grew up a Whig, he is astonishingly free from tendency to assume that "the truth lies somewhere in between." The truth lay where intellect and logic found it, and he was not abashed by clearness of outline.

This type of conservative is sometimes found fighting quite briskly for change; but if there is one thing by which he is distinguished, it is a trust in the methods of law. For him law is the embodiment of abstract justice; it is not "what the courts will decide tomorrow," or a calculation of the forces at work in society. A sentence from the First Inaugural Address will give us the conservative's view of pragmatic jurisprudence: "I do suggest that it will be much safer for all, both in official and private stations, to conform to and abide by all those acts which stand unrepealed, than to violate any of them, trusting to find impunity in having them held to be unconstitutional."[42] The essence of Lincoln's doctrine was not the seeking of a middle, but reform according to law; that is, reform according to definition. True conservatism can be intellectual in the same way as true classicism. It is one of the polar positions; and it deserves an able exponent as well as does its vivifying opposite, true radicalism.

41. Stern, *Writings*, p. 423.
42. *Ibid.*, p. 649.

After Lincoln had left the scene, the Republican Party, as we have noted, was unable to meet the test of victory. It turned quickly to the worship of Mammon, and with the exception of the ambiguous Theodore Roosevelt, it never found another leader. No one understood better than Lincoln that the party would have to succeed upon principle. He told his followers during the campaign of 1858: "nobody has ever expected me to be President. In my poor, lean, lank face nobody has even seen that any cabbages were sprouting out. These are disadvantages all, taken together, that the Republicans labor under. We have to fight this battle upon principle and upon principle alone."[43] For two generations this party lived upon the moral capital amassed during the anti-slavery campaign, but after that had been expended, and terrible issues had to be faced, it possessed nothing. It was less successful than the British Tories because it was either ignorant or ashamed of the good things it had to offer. Today it shows in advanced form that affliction which has overcome the "good elements" in all modern nations in the face of the bold and enterprising bad ones.

Let it be offered as a parting counsel that parties bethink themselves of how their chieftains speak. This is a world in which one often gets what one asks for more directly or more literally than one expects. If a leader asks only consequences, he will find himself involved in naked competition of forces. If he asks only circumstance, he will find himself intimidated against all vision. But if he asks for principle, he may get that, all tied up and complete, and though purchased at a price, paid for. Therefore it is of first importance whether a leader has the courage to define. Nowhere does a man's rhetoric catch up with him more completely than in the topics he chooses to win other men's assent.

---

43. Stern, *Writings*, p. 452.

Chapter V

SOME RHETORICAL ASPECTS OF GRAMMATICAL CATEGORIES

IN AN EARLIER part of this work we defined rhetoric as something which creates an informed appetition for the good. Such definition must recognize the rhetorical force of things existing outside the realm of speech; but since our concern is primarily with spoken rhetoric, which cannot be disengaged from certain patterns or regularities of language, we now turn our attention to the pressure of these formal patterns.

All students of language concede to it a certain public character. Insofar as it serves in communication, it is a publicly-agreed-upon thing; and when one passes the outer limits of the agreement, one abandons comprehensibility. Now rhetoric affects us primarily by setting forth images which inform and attract. Yet because this setting forth is accomplished through a public instrumentality, it is not free; it is tied more or less closely to the formalizations of usage. The more general and rigid of these formalizations we recognize as grammar, and we shall here speak of grammar as a system of forms of public speech. In the larger aspect, discourse is at once bound and free, and we are here interested to discover how the bound character affects our ability to teach and to persuade.

We soon realize that different ways of saying a thing denote different interests in saying it, or to take this in reverse as we do when we become conscious users of language, different interests in a matter will dictate different patterns of expression. Rhetoric in its practice is a matter of selection and arrangement, but conventional grammar imposes restraints upon both of these. All this amounts to saying what every sensitive user of language has sometimes felt; namely, that language is not a purely passive instrument, but that, owing to this public acceptance, while you are doing something with it, it is doing something with you, or with your intention.[1] It does not exactly fight back; rather it has a set of postures and balances which somehow modify your thrusts and holds. The sentence form is certainly one of these. You pour into it your meaning, and it deflects, and molds into certain shapes. The user of language must know how this counterpressure can be turned to the advantage of his general purpose. The failure of those who are careless, or insensitive, to the rhetoric of grammar is that they allow the counter force to impede their design, whereas a perspicacious use of it will forward the design. One cannot, for example, employ just any modifier to stand for a substantive or just any substantive to express a quality, or change a stabilized pattern of arrangement without a change in net effect, although some of these changes register but faintly. But style shows through an accumulation of small particulars, and the artist in language may ponder a long while, as Conrad is said to have done, over whether to describe a character as "penniless" or "without a penny."

In this approach, then, we are regarding language as a standard objective reality, analyzable into categories which have inherent potentialities. A knowledge of these objective potentialities can prevent a loss of force through friction. The friction we refer to occurs whenever a given unit of the system of grammar is tending to say one thing while the semantic meaning and the general organization are tending to say another. A language has certain abilities or even inclinations which

---

1. To mention a simple example, the sarcasm uttered as a pleasantry sometimes leaves a wound because its formal signification is not entirely removed by the intonation of the user or by the speech situation.

the wise user can draw into the service of his own rhetorical effort. Using a language may be compared to riding a horse; much of one's success depends upon an understanding of what it *can* and *will* do. Or to employ a different figure in illustration, there is a kind of use of language which goes against the grain as that grain is constituted by the categories, and there is a kind which facilitates the speaker's projection by going with it. Our task is an exploration of the congruence between well understood rhetorical objectives and the inherent character of major elements in modern English.

The problem of which category to begin with raises some questions. It is arguable that the rhetoric of any piece is dependent upon its total intention, and that consequently no single sentence can be appraised apart from the tendency of the whole discourse. Our position does not deny that, since we are assuming merely that within the greater effect there are lesser effects, cooperating well or ill. Having accepted that limitation, it seems permissible for us to begin with the largest unit of grammar, which is the sentence. We shall take up first the sentence as such and then discriminate between formal types of sentences.

Because a sentence form exists in most if not all languages, there is some ground to suppose that it reflects a necessary operation of the mind, and this means not simply of the mind as psychologically constituted but also as logically constrained.

It is evident that when the mind frames a sentence, it performs the basic intellectual operation of analysis and re-synthesis. In this complete operation the mind is taking two or more classes and uniting them at least to the extent at which they share in a formal unity. The unity itself, built up through many such associations, comes to have an existence all its own, as we shall see. It is the repeated congruence in experience or in the imagination of such classes as "sun-heat," "snow-cold," which establishes the pattern, but our point is that the pattern once established can become disciplinary in itself and compel us to look for meaning within the formal unity it imposes. So it is natural for us to perceive through a primitive analysis the compresence of sun and hot weather, and to combine these into the unity "the sun is hot"; but the articulation represented by this joining now becomes a thing in itself, which can be grasped before the meaning of its component parts is evident. Accordingly, although sentences are supposed to grow out of meanings, we can have sentences before meanings are apparent, and this is indeed the central point of our rhetoric of grammar. When we thus grasp the scope of the pattern before we interpret the meaning of the components, we are being affected by grammatical system.

I should like to put this principle to a supreme sort of test by using a few lines of highly modern verse. In Allen Tate's poem "The Subway" we find the following:

> I am become geometries, and glut
> Expansions like a blind astronomer
> Dazed, while the wordless heavens bulge and reel
> In the cold reverie of an idiot.

I do not propose to interpret this further than to say that the features present of word classification and word position cause us to look for meaning along certain lines. It seems highly probable that we shall have to exercise much imagination to fit our classes together with meaning as they are fitted by formal classification and sentence order ("I am become geometries"); yet it remains true that we take in the first line as a formal predication; and I do not think that this formal character could ever be separated entirely from the substance in an interpretation. Once we gain admission of that point with regard to a sentence, some rhetorical status for grammar has been definitely secured.

In total rhetorical effect the sentence seems to be peculiarly "the thing said," whereas all other elements are "the things named." And accordingly the right to utter a sentence is one of the very greatest liberties; and we are entitled to little wonder that freedom of utterance should be, in every society, one of the most contentious and ill-defined rights. The liberty to impose this formal unity is a liberty to handle the world, to remake it, if only a little, and to hand it to others in a shape which may influence their actions. It is interesting to speculate whether the Greeks did not, for this very reason, describe the man clever at speech as δεινός, an epithet meaning, in addition tc "clever," "fearful" and "terrible." The sentence through its office of assertion is a force adding itself to the forces of the world, and therefore the man clever with his sentences—which is to say with his combinations—was regarded with that uneasiness which we feel in the presence of power. The changes wrought by sentences are changes in the world rather than in the physical earth, but it is to be remembered that changes in the world bring about changes in the earth. Thus this practice of yoking together classes of the world, of saying "Charles is King" or "My country is God's country" is a unique rhetorical fact which we have to take into account, although it stands somewhat prior to our main discussion.

As we turn now to the different formal types of sentences, we shall follow the traditional grammatical classification and discuss the rhetorical inclination of each in turn.

Through its form, the simple sentence tends to emphasize the discreteness of phenomena within the structural unity. To be more specific, its pattern of subject-verb-object or complement, without major competing elements, leaves our attention fixed upon the classes involved: "Charles is King." The effect remains when the simple sentence compounds its subject and predicate: "Peaches and cantaloupes grew in abundance"; "Men and boys hunted and fished." The single subject-predicate frame has the broad sense of listing or itemizing, and the list becomes what the sentence is about semantically.

Sentences of this kind are often the unconscious style of one who sees the world as a conglomerate of things, like the child; sometimes they are the conscious style of one who seeks to present certain things as eminent against a background of matter uniform or flat. One can imagine, for example, the simple sentence "He never worked" coming after a long and tedious recital which it is supposed to highlight. Or one can imagine the sentence "The world is round" leaping out of a context with which it contrasts in meaning, in brevity, or in sententiousness.

There is some descriptive value in saying that the simple sentence is the most "logical" type of sentence because, like the simple categorical proposition, it has this function of relating two classes. This fact, combined with its usual brevity and its structural simplicity, makes it a useful sentence for beginnings and endings (of important meaning-groups, not so much of formal introductions and conclusions). It is a sentence of unclouded perspective, so to speak. Nothing could be more beautifully anticipatory than Burke's "The proposition is peace."

At the very minimum, we can affirm that the simple sentence tends to throw subject and predicate classes into relief by the structure it presents them in; that the two-part categorical form of its copulation indicates a positive mood on the part of the user, and that its brevity often induces a generality of approach, which is an aid to perspicuous style. These opportunities are found out by the speaker or writer who senses the need for some synoptic or dramatic spot in his discourse. Thus when he selects the simple sentence, he is going "with the grain"; he is putting the objective form to work for him.

The complex sentence has a different potentiality. Whereas the simple sentence emphasizes through its form the co-existence of classes (and it must be already apparent that we regard "things existing or occurring" as a class where the predicate consists only of a verb), the complex sentence emphasizes a more complex relationship; that is to say, it reflects another kind of discriminating activity, which does not stop with seeing discrete classes as co-existing, but distinguishes them according to rank or value, or places them in an order of cause and effect. "Rome fell because valor declined" is the utterance of a reflective mind because the conjunction of parts depends on something ascertainable by the intellect but not by simple perception. This is evidence that the complex sentence does not appear until experience has undergone some refinement by the mind. Then, because it goes beyond simple observation and begins to perceive things like causal principle, or begins to grade things according to a standard of interest, it brings in the notion of dependence to supplement that of simple togetherness. And consequently the complex sentence will be found nearly always to express some sort of hierarchy, whether spatial, moral, or causal, with its subordinate members describing the lower orders. In simple-sentence style we would write: "Tragedy began in Greece. It is the highest form of literary art." There is no disputing that these sentences, in this sequence, could have a place in mature expression. But they do not have the same effect as "Tragedy, which is the highest form of literary art, began in Greece" or "Tragedy, which began in Greece, is the highest form of literary art." What has occurred is the critical process of subordination. The two ideas have been transferred from a conglomerate to an articulated unity, and the very fact of subordination makes inevitable the emergence of a focus of interest. Is our passage about the highest form of literary art or about the cultural history of Greece? The form of the complex sentence makes it unnecessary to waste any words in explicit assertion of that. Here it is plain that grammatical form is capital upon which we can draw, provided that other necessities have been taken care of.

To see how a writer of consummate sensibility toward expression-forms proceeded, let us take a fairly typical sentence from Henry James:

Merton Densher, who passed the best hours of each night at the office of his newspaper, had at times, during the day, a sense, or at least an appearance, of leisure, in accordance with which he was not infrequently to be met, in different parts of the town, at moments when men of business were hidden from the public eye.[2]

Leaving aside the phrases, which are employed by James in extension and refinement of the same effect, we see here three dependent clauses used to explain the contingencies of "Merton Densher had an appearance of leisure." These clauses have the function of surrounding the central statement in such a fashion that we have an intricate design of thought characterized by involution, or the emergence of one detail out of another. James' famous practice of using the dependent clause not only for qualification, but for the qualification of qualification, and in some cases for the qualification of qualification of qualification, indicates a persistent sorting out of experience expressive of the highly civilized mind. Perhaps the leading quality of the civilized mind is that it is sophisticated as to causes and effects (also as to other contiguities); and the complex sentence, required to give these a scrupulous ordering, is its natural vehicle.

At the same time the spatial form of ordering to which the complex sentence lends itself makes it a useful tool in scientific analysis, and one can find brilliant examples of it in the work of scientists who have been skillful in communication. When T. H. Huxley, for instance, explains a piece of anatomy, the complex sentence is the frame of explanation. In almost every sentence it will be observed that he is focussing interest upon one part while keeping its relationship—spatial or causal— clear with reference to surrounding parts. In Huxley's expository prose, therefore, one finds the dominant sentence type to consist of a main clause at the beginning followed by a series of dependent clauses which fill in these facts of relationship. We may follow the pattern of the sentences in his account of the protoplasm of the common nettle:

2. *The Wings of the Dove* (Modern Library ed., New York, 1937), p. 53.

Each stinging-needle tapers from a broad base to a slender summit, which, though rounded at the end, is of such microscopic fineness that it readily penetrates, and breaks off in, the skin. The whole hair consists of a very delicate outer case of wood, closely applied to the inner surface of which is a layer of semi-fluid matter full of innumerable granules of extreme minuteness. This semifluid lining is protoplasm, which thus constitutes a kind of bag, full of limpid liquid, and roughly corresponding in form with the interior of the hair which it fills.[3]

This is, of course, the "loose" sentence of traditional rhetorical analysis, and it has no dramatic force; yet it is for this very reason adapted to the scientist's purpose.[4] The rhetorical adaptation shows in the accommodation of a little hierarchy of details.

This appears to be the sentence of a developed mentality also, because it is created through a patient, disciplined observation, and not through impression, as the simple sentence can be. To the infant's mind, as William James observed in a now famous passage, the world is a "buzzing, blooming confusion," and to the immature mind much older it often appears something done in broad, uniform strokes. But to the mind of a trained scientist it has to appear a cosmos—else, no science. So in Huxley the objective world is presented as a series of details, each of which has its own cluster of satellites in the form of minor clauses. This is the way the world has to be reported when our objective is maximum perception and minimum desire to obtrude or influence.

Henry James was explaining with a somewhat comparable interest a different kind of world, in which all sorts of human and non-material forces are at work, and he tried with extreme

3. "On the Physical Basis of Life," *Lay Sermons, Addresses and Reviews* (New York, 1883), pp. 123–24.

4. On this point it is pertinent to cite Huxley's remark in another lay sermon, "On the Study of Zoology" (*ibid.*, p. 110): "I have a strong impression that the better a discourse is, as an oration, the worse it is as a lecture."

conscientiousness to measure them. In that process of quantification and qualification the complex sentence was often
brought by him to an extraordinary height of ramification.

In summation, then, the complex sentence is the branching
sentence, or the sentence with parts growing off other parts.
Those who have used it most properly have performed a second act of analysis, in which the objects of perception, after
being seen discretely, are put into a ranked structure. This
type of sentence imposes the greatest demand upon the reader
because it carries him farthest into the reality existing outside
self. This point will take on importance as we turn to the compound sentence.

The structure of the compound sentence often reflects a
simple artlessness—the uncritical pouring together of simple
sentences, as in the speech of Huckleberry Finn. The child
who is relating an adventure is likely to make it a flat recital
of conjoined simple predications, because to him the important fact is that the things were, not that they can be read to
signify this or that. His even juxtapositions are therefore sometimes amusing, for now and then he will produce a coordination that unintentionally illuminates. This would, of course,
be a result of lack of control over the rhetoric of grammar.

On the other hand, the compound sentence can be a very
"mature" sentence when its structure conforms with a settled
view of the world. The latter possibility will be seen as we
think of the balance it presents. When a sentence consists of
two main clauses we have two predications of similar structure bidding for our attention. Our first supposal is that this
produces a sentence of unusual tension, with two equal parts
(and of course sometimes more than two equal parts) in a
sort of competition. Yet it appears on fuller acquaintance that
this tension is a tension of stasis, and that the compound sentence has, in practice, been markedly favored by periods of
repose like that of the Eighteenth century. There is congenial-
ity between its internal balance and a concept of the world as
an equilibrium of forces. As a general rule, it appears that

whereas the complex sentence favors the presentation of the world as a system of facts or as a dynamism, the compound sentence favors the presentation of it in a more or less philosophical picture. This world as a philosophical cosmos will have to be a sort of compensatory system. We know from other evidences that the Eighteenth century loved to see things in balance; in fact, it required the idea of balance as a foundation for its institutions. Quite naturally then, since motives of this kind reach into expression-forms, this was the age of masters of the balanced sentence—Dryden, Johnson, Gibbon, and others, the *genre* of whose style derives largely from this practice of compounding. Often the balance which they achieved was more intricate than simple conjunction of main clauses because they balanced lesser elements too, but the informing impulse was the same. That impulse was the desire for counterpoise, which was one of the powerful motives of their culture.

In this pattern of balance, various elements are used in the offsettings. Thus when one attends closely to the meanings of the balanced parts, one finds these compounds recurring: an abstract statement is balanced (in a second independent clause) by a more concrete expression of the same thing; a fact is balanced by its causal explanation; a statement of positive mode is balanced by one of negative mode; a clause of praise is balanced by a clause of qualified censure; a description of one part is balanced by a description of a contrasting part, and so on through a good many conventional pairings. Now in these collocations cause and effect and other relationships are presented, yet the attempt seems not so much to explore reality as to clothe it in decent form. Culture is a delicate reconciliation of opposites, and consequently a man who sees the world through the eyes of a culture makes effort in this direction. We know that the world of Eighteenth century culture was a rationalist world, and in a rationalist world everything must be "accounted for." The virtue of the compound sentence is that its second part gives "the other half," so to speak. As the pattern works out, every fact has its cause; every virtue is compensated for by a vice; every excursion into generality must be made up for by attention to concrete circumstances and vice versa. The perfection of this art form is found in Johnson and Gibbon, where such pairings occur with a frequency which has given rise to the phrase "the balanced style." When Gibbon, for example, writes of religion in the Age of the Antonines: "The superstition of the people was not embittered by any mixture of theological rancour; nor was it confined by the chains of any speculative system,"[5] we have almost the feeling that the case of religion has been settled by this neat artifice of expression. This is a "just" view of affairs, which sees both sides and leaves a kind of balanced account. It looks somewhat subjective, or at least humanized; it gives us the gross world a little tidied up by thought. Often, moreover, this balance of structure together with the act of saying a thing equivocally—in the narrower etymological sense of that word—suggests the finality of art. This will be found true of many of the poetical passages of the King James Bible, although these come from an earlier date. "The heavens declare the glory of God; and the firmament sheweth his handiwork"; "Man cometh forth as a flower and is cut down; he fleeth also as a shadow and continueth not." By thus stating the matter in two ways, through balanced clauses, the sentence achieves a degree of formal completeness missing in sentences where the interest is in mere assertion. Generally speaking the balanced compound sentence, by the very contrivedness of its structure, suggests something formed above the welter of experience, and this form, as we have by now substantially said, transfers something of itself to the meaning. In declaring that the compound sentence may seem subjective, we are not saying that it is arbitrary, its correspondence being with the philosophical interpretation rather than with the factual real-

---

5. *Decline and Fall of the Roman Empire* (Bury's ed., London, 1900), I, 28.

ity. Thus if the complex sentence is about the world, the compound sentence is about our idea about the world, into which some notion of compensation forces itself. One notices that even Huxley, when he draws away from his simple expositions of fact and seeks play for his great powers of persuasion, begins to compound his sentences. On the whole, the compound sentence conveys that completeness and symmetry which the world *ought* to have, and which we manage to get, in some measure, into our most satisfactory explanations of it. It is most agreeable to those ages and those individuals who feel that they have come to terms with the world, and are masters in a domain. But understandably enough, in a world which has come to be centrifugal and infinite, as ours has become since the great revolutions, it tends to seem artificial and mechanical in its containment.

Since the difference between sentence and clause is negligible as far as the issues of this subject are concerned, we shall next look at the word, and conclude with a few remarks on some lesser combinations. This brings up at once the convention of parts of speech. Here again I shall follow the traditional classification, on the supposition that categories to which usage is referred for correction have accumulated some rhetorical force, whatever may be said for the merits of some other and more scientific classification.

The Noun

It is difficult not to feel that both usage and speculation agree on the rhetorical quality of nouns. The noun derives its special dignity from being a *name* word, and names persist, in spite of all the cautions of modern semanticists, in being thought of as words for substances. We apprehend the significance of that when we realize that in the ancient philosophical regimen to which the West is heir, and which influences our thought far more than we are aware at any one moment, substances are assigned a higher degree of being than actions or qualities. Substance is that which primordially *is*, and one may doubt whether recent attempts to revolutionize both ontology and grammar have made any impression at all against this feeling. For that reason a substantive comes to us as something that is peculiarly fulfilled;[6] or it is like a piece in a game which has superior powers of movement and capture. The fact that a substantive is the word in a sentence which the other words are "about" in various relationships gives it a superior status.[7]

Nouns then express things whose being is completed, not whose being is in process, or whose being depends upon some other being. And that no doubt accounts for the feeling that when one is using nouns, one is manipulating the symbols of a self-subsistent reality.[8] There seems little doubt that an ancient metaphysical system, grown to be an *habitus* of the mind through long acceptance, gives the substantive word a prime status, and this fact has importance when we come to compare the noun with the adjective in power to convince by making real. Suffice it to say here that the noun, whether it be a pointer to things that one can touch and see, as *apple, bird, sky*, or to the more or less hypothetical substances such as *fairness, spook, nothingness*, by rule stands at the head of things and is ministered to by the other parts of speech and by combinations.

---

6. Cf. Kenneth Burke, *Attitudes Toward History* (New York, 1937), I, 82–83: "Looking over the titles of books written by Huysmans, who went *from* naturalism, *through* Satanism, *to* Catholicism, we find that his titles of the naturalistic period are with one exception nouns, all those of the transitional period are prepositions actually or in quality ("A-Vau-l'Eau," "En Rade," "A Rebours," "La Bas," "En Route") and all in his period of Catholic realism are nouns."

7. In German all nouns are regularly capitalized, and the German word for noun substantive is *Hauptwort* or "head word." In this grammatical vision the noun becomes a sort of "captain" in the sentence.

8. Cf. Aristotle, *Rhetoric*, 1410 b: "And let this be our fundamental principle: for the receiving of information with ease, is naturally pleasing to all; and nouns are significant of something; so that all those nouns whatsoever which produce knowledge in the mind, are most pleasing."

The Adjective

The adjective is, by the principle of determination just reviewed, a word of secondary status and force. Its burden is an attribute, or something added. In the order of being to which reference has been made, the noun can exist without the adjective, but not the adjective without the noun. Thus we can have "men" without having "excellent men"; but we cannot have "excellent" without having something (if only something understood) to receive the attribution. There are very practical rhetorical lessons to be drawn from this truth. Since adjectives express attributes which are conceptually dispensable to the substances wherein they are present, the adjective tends to be a supernumerary. Long before we are aware of this fact through analysis, we sense it through our resentment of any attempt to gain maximum effect through the adjective. Our intuition of speech seems to tell us that the adjective is question-begging; that is to say, if the thing to be expressed is real, it will be expressed through a substantive; if it is expressed mainly through adjectives, there is something defective in its reality, since it has gone for secondary support.[9] If someone should say to us, "Have some white milk," we must suppose either that the situation is curious, other kinds of milk being available, or that the speaker is trying to impose upon us by a piece of persiflage. Again, a mountain is a mountain without being called "huge"; if we have to call it huge, there is some defect in the original image which is being made up. Of course there are speech situations in which such modifiers do make a useful contribution, but as a general rule, to be applied with discretion, a style is stronger when it depends mainly upon substantives sharp enough to convey their own attributes.

9. Compare the following passage by Carl Sandburg in "Trying to Write," *Atlantic Monthly*, Vol. 186, No. 3 (September, 1950), p. 33: "I am still studying verbs and the mystery of how they connect nouns. I am more suspicious of adjectives than at any other time in all my born days."

Furthermore, because the class of the adjective contains so many terms of dialectical import, such as *good, evil, noble, base, useful, useless,* there is bound to exist an initial suspicion of all adjectives. (Even when they are the positive kind, as is true with most limiting adjectives, there lurk the questions "Who made up the statistics?" and "How were they gathered?") The dialectical adjective is too often a "fighting word" to be used casually. Because in its very origin it is the product of disputation, one is far from being certain in advance of assent to it. How would you wish to characterize the world? If you wish to characterize it as "round," you will win a very general assent, although not a universal one. But if you wish, with the poet, to characterize it as "sorry," you take a position in respect to which there are all sorts of contrary positions. In strictest thought one might say that every noun contains its own analysis, but an adjective applied to a noun is apparatus brought in from the outside; and the result is the object slightly "fictionized." Since adjectives thus initiate changes in the more widely received substantive words, one has to have permission of his audience to talk in adjectives. Karl Shapiro seems to have had something like this in mind in the following passage from his *Essay on Rime:*

> for the tyrannical epithet
> Relies upon the adjective to produce
> The image; and no serious construction
> In rime can build upon the modifier.[10]

One of the common mistakes of the inexperienced writer, in prose as well as poetry, is to suppose that the adjective can set the key of a discourse. Later he learns what Shapiro indicates, that nearly always the adjective has to have the way prepared for it. Otherwise, the adjective introduced before its noun collapses for want of support. There is a perceptible difference between "the irresponsible conduct of the opposi-

---

10. *Essay on Rime* (New York, 1945), p. 43, ll. 1224–1227.

tion with regard to the Smith bill" and "the conduct of the
opposition with regard to the Smith bill has been irresponsible," which is accounted for in part by the fact that the adjective comes after the substantive has made its firm impression. In like manner we are prepared to receive Henley's

> Out of the night that covers me,
> Black as the Pit from pole to pole

because "night" has preceded "black." I submit that if the
poem had begun "Black as . . ." it would have lost a great deal
of its rhetorical force because of the inherent character of the
opening word. The adjective would have been felt presumptuous, as it were, and probably no amount of supplementation
could have overcome this unfortunate effect.

I shall offer one more example to show that costly mistakes
in emphasis may result from supposing that the adjective can
compete with the noun. This one came under my observation,
and has remained with me as a classical instance of rhetorical
ineptitude. On a certain university campus "Peace Week" was
being observed, and a prominent part of the program was a
series of talks. The object of these talks was to draw attention
to those forces which seemed to be leading mankind toward
a third world war. One of the speakers undertook to point out
the extent to which the Western nations, and especially the
United States, were at fault. He declared that a chief source
of the bellicose tendency of the United States was its "proud
rectitude," and it is this expression which I wish to examine
critically. The fault of the phrase is that it makes "rectitude"
the villain of the piece, whereas sense calls for making "pride."
If we are correct in assigning the substantive a greater intrinsic weight, then it follows that "rectitude" exerts the greater force here. But rectitude is not an inciter of wars; it is
rather that rectitude which is made rigid or unreasonable by
pride which may be a factor in the starting of wars, and pride
is really the provoking agent. For the most fortunate effect,

then, the grammatical relationship should be reversed, and we should have "rectitude" modifying "pride." But since the accident of linguistic development has not provided it with an adjective form of equivalent meaning, let us try "pride of rectitude." This is not the best expression imaginable, but it is somewhat better since it turns "proud" into a substantive and demotes "rectitude" to a place in a prepositional phrase. The weightings are now more in accordance with meaning: what grammar had anomalously made the chief word is now properly tributary, and we have a closer delineation of reality. As it was, the audience went away confused and uninspired, and I have thought of this ever since as a situation in which a little awareness of the rhetoric of grammar—there were other instances of imperceptive usage—could have turned a merely well-intentioned speech into an effective one.

Having laid down this relationship between adjective and substantive as a principle, we must not ignore the real or seeming exceptions. For the alert reader will likely ask, what about such combinations as "new potatoes," "drunk men," "a warlike nation"? Are we prepared to say that in each of these the substantive gets the major attention, that we are more interested in "potatoes" than in their being "new," in "men" than their being "drunk," and so forth? Is that not too complacent a rule about the priority of the substantive over the adjective?

We have to admit that there are certain examples in which the adjective may eclipse the substantive. This may occur (1) when one's intonation (or italics) directs attention to the modifier: "*white* horses"; "*five* dollars, not four." (2) when there is a striking clash of meaning between the adjective and the substantive, such that one gives a second thought to the modifier: "a murderous smile"; "a gentleman gambler." (3) when the adjective is naturally of such exciting associations that it has become a sort of traditional introduction to matter of moment: "a warlike nation"; "a desperate deed"; etc. Having admitted these possibilities of departure from the rule, we still feel right in saying that the rule has some force. It will be found useful in cases which are doubtful, which are the cases where no strong semantic or phonetic considerations override the grammatical pattern. In brief, when the immediate act of our mind does not tell us whether an expression should be in this form or the other, the principle of the relationship of adjective and substantive may settle the matter with an insight which the particular instance has not called forth.

The Adverb

The adverb is distinguished from the other parts of speech by its superior mobility; roughly speaking, it can locate itself anywhere in the sentence, and this affords a clue to its character. "Certainly the day is warm"; "The day certainly is warm"; "The day is certainly warm"; "The day is warm certainly" are all "normal" utterances. This superior mobility, amounting to a kind of detachment, makes the adverb peculiarly a word of judgment. Here the distinction between the adverb and the adjective seems to be that the latter depends more upon public agreement and less upon private intention in its applications. It is a matter of common observation that the adverb is used frequently to express an attitude which is the speaker's projection of himself. "Surely the war will end soon" is not, for example, a piece of objective reporting but an expression of subjective feeling. We of course recognize degrees of difference in the personal or subjective element. Thomas Carlyle is much given to the use of the adverb, and when we study his adverbs in context, we discover that they are often little more than explosions of feeling. They are employed to make more positive, abrupt, sensational, or intense whatever his sentence is otherwise saying. Indeed, take from Carlyle his adverbs and one robs him of that great hortatory sweep which makes him one of the great preachers in English literature. On the other hand Henry James, although given to this use to comparable extent, gets a different effect from his adverbs. With him they are the exponents of scrupulous or meticulous feeling; they are often in fact words of definite measure. When James says "fully" or "quickly" or "bravely" he is usually expressing a definite perception, and sometimes the adverb will have its own phrasal modifier to give it the proper direction or limitation of sense. Therefore James' adverbs, instead of having a merely expletive force, as do many of Carlyle's, tend to integrate themselves with his more objective description. All this amounts to saying that adverbial "judgments" can be differently based; and the use of the adverb will affect a style accordingly.

The caution against presumptuous use of the adjective can be repeated with somewhat greater force for the adverb. It is the most tempting of all the parts of speech to question-beg with. It costs little, for instance, to say "certainly," "surely," or even "terribly," "awfully," "undoubtedly"; but it often costs a great deal to create the picture upon which these words are a justifiable verdict. Asking the reader to accept them upon the strength of simple assertion is obviously a form of taking without earning. We realize that a significant part of every speech situation is the character of the speaker; and there are characters who can risk an unproved "certainly" or "undoubtedly." They bring to the speech situation a kind of ethical proof which accentuates their language. Carlyle's reflective life was so intense, as we know from *Sartor Resartus* and other sources, that it wins for him a certain right to this asseverative style. As a general rule, though, it will be found that those who are most entitled to this credit use it least, which is to say, they prefer to make their demonstrations. We point out in summary that the adverb is frequently dependent upon the character of its user, and that, since it is often the qualifier of a qualifier, it may stand at one more remove from what we have defined as the primary symbol. This is why beginners should use it least—should use it only after they have demonstrated that they can get their results by other means.

The Verb

The verb is regularly ranked with the noun in force, and it seems that these two parts of speech express the two aspects under which we habitually see phenomena, that of determinate things and that of actions or states of being. Between them the two divide up the world at a pretty fundamental depth; and it is a commonplace of rhetorical instruction that a style made up predominantly of nouns and verbs will be a vigorous style. These are the symbols of the prime entities, words of stasis and words of movement (even when the verb is said to express a "state of being," we accept that as a kind of modal action, a process of going on, or having existential quality), which set forth the broad circumstances of any subject of discussion. This truth is supported by the facts that the substantive is the heart of a grammatical subject and the verb of a grammatical predicate.

When we pass beyond the matter of broad categorization to look at the verb's possibilities, we find the greatest need of instruction to lie in the verb epithet. It may be needless to impress any literate person with the verb's relative importance, but it is necessary to point out, even to some practiced writers, that the verb itself can modify the action it asserts, or, so to put it, can carry its own epithet. Looking at the copious supply of verbs in English, we often find it possible to choose one so selective in meaning that no adverb is needed to accompany it. If we wish to assert that "the man moves *quickly*," we can say, depending on the tone of our passage and the general signification, that he *hastens, rushes, flies, scrambles, speeds, tears, races, bolts,* to name only a few. If we wish to assert that a man is not telling the truth, we have the choice of *lies, prevaricates, falsifies, distorts, exaggerates,* and some others. As this may seem to treat the matter at too didactic a level, let us generalize by saying that there is such a thing as the characterizing verb, and that there is no telling how many words could have been saved, how many passages could have dispensed with a lumbering and perhaps inaccurate adverb, if this simple truth about the verb were better appreciated. The best writers of description and narration know it. Mark Twain's most vivid passages are created largely through a frequent and perceptive use of the verb epithet. Turn to almost any page of *Life on the Mississippi:*

> Ship channels are buoyed and lighted, and therefore it is a comparatively easy undertaking to learn to run them; clear-water rivers, with gravel bottoms, change their channels very gradually, and therefore one needs to learn them but once; but piloting becomes another matter when you apply it to vast streams like the Mississippi and the Missouri, whose alluvial banks cave and change constantly, whose snags are always hunting up new quarters, whose sand-bars are never at rest, whose channels are forever dodging and shirking, and whose obstructions must be confronted in all nights and all weathers without the aid of a single lighthouse or a single buoy, for there is neither light nor buoy to be found anywhere in all this three or four thousand miles of villainous river.[11]

Here there occurs not just action, but expressive action, to which something is contributed by Twain's subtle appreciation of modal variations in the verb.

There is a rough parallelism between the use of the complex sentence, with its detail put away in subordinate constructions, and the use of the verb epithet. In both instances the user has learned to dispense with a second member of equal or nearly equal weight in order to get an effect. As the adverbial qualification is fused with the verb, so in lesser degree, of course, is the detail of the complex sentence fused with its principal assertion. These devices of economy and compression, although they may be carried to a point at which the style seems forced and unnatural, are among the most important means of rhetoric.

---

11. *Life on the Mississippi* (New York, 1903), p. 73.

The Conjunction

The conjunction, in its simple role as joiner, seems not to have much character, yet its use expresses of relatedness of things, which is bound to have signification. As either coordinator or subordinator of entities, it puts the world into a condition of mutual relationship through which a large variety of ideas may be suggested. From the different ways in which this relationship is expressed, the reader will consciously and even unconsciously infer different things. Sometimes the simple "and . . . and" coordination is the expression of childlike mentality, as we saw in our discussion of the compound sentence. On the other hand, in a different speech situation it can produce a quite different effect: readers of the King James version of the Bible are aware of how the "and" which joins long sequences of verses sets up a kind of expectancy which is peculiarly in keeping with sacred text. One gets the feeling from the reiteration of "and" that the story is confirmed and inevitable; there are no contingencies, and everything happens with the double assurance of something foretold. When this pattern is dropped, as it is in a recent "American" version of the Bible, the text collapses into a kind of news story.

The frequent use of "but" to join the parts of a compound sentence seems to indicate a habit of mind. It is found congenial by those who take a "balanced view," or who are uneasy over an assertion until it has been qualified or until some recognition has been made of its negative. Its influence is in the direction of the cautious or pedantic style because it makes this sort of disjunction, whereas "and" generously joins everything up.

Since conjunctions are usually interpreted as giving the plot of one's thought, it is essential to realize that they have implicit meanings. They usually come at points where a pause is natural, and there is a temptation, if one may judge by indulgence in the habit, to lean upon the first one that comes to mind without reflecting critically upon its significance, so that although the conjunction may formally connect at this point, its semantic meaning does not aid in making the connection precise. A common instance of this fault is the casual interchange of "therefore" and "thus." "Therefore" means "in consequence of," but "thus" means "in this manner" and so indicates that some manner has already been described. "Hence" may take the place of "therefore" but "thus" may not. "Also" is a connective used with unimaginative regularity by poor speakers and writers, for whom it seems to signalize the next thought coming. Yet in precise meaning "also" signifies only a mechanical sort of addition such as we have in listing one item after another. To signalize the extension of an idea, "moreover" is usually more appropriate than "also." Although "while" is often used in place of "whereas" to mean "on the other hand," it has its other duty of signifying "at the same time." "Whereas," despite its pedantic or legalistic overtone, will be preferred in passages where precise relationship is the governing consideration. On the whole it would seem that the average writer suffers, in the department, from nothing more than poverty of vocabulary. What he does (what every writer does to some extent) is to keep on hand a small set of conjunctions and to use them in a sort of rotation without giving attention to how their distinctive meanings could further his purpose.

The Preposition

The preposition too is a word expressing relationships, but this definition gives only a faint idea of its great resources. When the false rules about the preposition have been set aside, it is seen that this is a tremendously inventive word. Like the adverb, it is a free rover, standing almost anywhere; it is constantly entering into combinations with verbs and nouns, in which it may direct, qualify, intensify, or even add something quite new to the meaning; at other times it combines with some other preposition to produce an indispensable idiom. It has given us "get out," "put over," "come across," "eat up," "butt in," "off of," "in between," and many other expressions without which English, especially on the vital colloquial level, would be poorer indeed. Thornton Wilder maintains that it is in this extremely free use of the preposition that modern American English shows its superiority over British English. Such bold use of prepositional combinations gives to American English a certain flavor of the grand style, which British English has not had since the seventeenth century. Melville, an author working peculiarly on his own, is characterized in style by this imaginative use of the preposition.

Considered with reference to principle, the preposition seems to do what the adverb does, but to do it with a kind of substantive force. "Groundward," for example, seems weak beside "toward the ground," "lengthwise" beside "along the length of," or "centrally" beside "in the center of." The explanation may well lie in the preposition's characteristic position; as a regular orderer of nouns and of verbs, it takes upon itself something of their solidity of meaning. "What is that for?" and "Where did you send it to?" lose none of their force through being terminated by these brief words of relationship.

The Phrase

It will not be necessary to say much about the phrase because its possibilities have been fairly well covered by our discussion of the noun and adjective. One qualifying remark about the force of the prepositional phrase, however, deserves making. The strength normally found in the preposition can be greatly diminished by connection with an abstract noun. That is to say, when the terminus of the preposition is lacking in vigor or concreteness, the whole expression may succumb to vagueness, in which cases the single adjective or adverb will be stronger by comparison. Thus the idea conveyed by "lazy" is largely frustrated by "of a lazy disposition";

that of "mercenary" by "of a mercenary character"; that of "deep" by "of depth," and so on.

After the prepositional phrase, the most important phrasal combination to examine, from the standpoint of rhetorical usages, is the participial phrase. We could infer this truth from the fact alone that the Greeks made a very extensive use of the participle, as every student of that marvellous language knows. Greek will frequently use a participle where English employs a dependent clause or even a full sentence, so that the English expression "the man who is carrying a spear" would be in Greek "the spear carrying man"; "the one who spoke" would be "the one having spoken" and further accordingly, with even more economy of language than these examples indicate. I am disposed to think that the Greeks developed this habit because they were very quick to see opportunities of subordination. The clarity and subtlety of the Greek language derives in no small part from this highly "organized" character, in which auxiliary thoughts are compactly placed in auxiliary structures, where they permit the central thought to emerge more readily. In English the auxiliary status of the participle (recognized formally through its classification as an adjective) is not always used to like advantage.

One consequence of this is that although English intonation and normal word order tend to make the last part of a sentence the most emphatic, unskillful writers sometimes lose this emphasis by concluding a sentence with a participial phrase. We may take as examples "He returned home in September, having been gone for a year"; and "Having been gone for a year, he returned home in September." The second of these puts the weightier construction in the emphatic position. Of course the matter of their relative merit cannot be separated from their purpose; there are sentences whose total meanings are best served by a *retardo* or *diminuendo* effect at the end, and for such closes the participial phrase is well suited for reasons already given. But in the majority of utterances it contributes best by modifying at some internal position, or by expressing some detail or some condition at the beginning of the sentence. The latter use may be quite effective in climactic orderings, and it will be found that journalists have virtually stereotyped this opening for their "lead" sentences: "Threatened with an exhausted food supply by the strike, hospitals today made special arrangements for the delivery of essentials"; "Reaching a new high for seven weeks, the stock market yesterday pushed into new territory." This form is a successful if often crude result of effort toward compact and dramatic presentation.

But to summarize our observations on the participial phrase in English: It is formally a weak member of the grammatical family; but it is useful for economy, for shaded effects, and sometimes the phrase will contain words whose semantic force makes us forget that they are in a secondary construction. Perhaps it is enough to say that the mature writer has learned more things that can be done with the participle, but has also learned to respect its limitations.

In Conclusion

I can imagine being told that this chapter is nothing more than an exposition of prejudices, and that every principle discussed here can be defied. I would not be surprised if that were proved through single examples, or small sets of examples. But I would still hazard that if these show certain tendencies, my examples show stronger ones, and we have to remember that there is such a thing as a vector of forces in language too. Even though an effect may sometimes be obtained by crowding or even breaking a rule, the lines of force are still there, to be used by the skillful writer scientifically, and grammar is a kind of scientific nomenclature. Beyond this, of course, he will use them according to art, where he will be guided by his artistic intuition, and by the residual cautions of his experience.

In the long view a due respect for the canons of grammar seems a part of one's citizenship. One does not remain uncritical; but one does "go along." It has proved impossible to show that grammar is determined by the "best people," or by the pedants, or by any other presumptive authority, and this is more reason for saying that it incorporates the people as a whole. Therefore the attitude of unthinking adoption and the attitude of personal defiance are both dubious, because they look away from the point where issues, whenever they appear, will be decided. That point seems to be some communal sense about the fitness of a word or a construction for what has communal importance, and this indicates at least some suprapersonal basis. Much evidence could be offered to show that language is something which is born psychological but is ever striving to become logical. At this task of making it more logical everybody works more or less. Like the political citizenship defined by Aristotle, language citizenship makes one a potential magistrate, or one empowered to decide. The work is best carried on, however, by those who are aware that language must have some connection with the intelligential world, and that is why one must think about the rhetorical nature even of grammatical categories.

Chapter VI

MILTON'S HEROIC PROSE

THERE ARE many who have wished that Milton were living at this hour, but not all have taken into account the fact that his great polemical writings demand an heroic kind of attention which modern education does not discipline the majority of our citizens to give. Even in the last century W. E. Channing was moved to lament "the fastidiousness and effeminacy of modern readers" when faced with Milton's prose writings. He went on to say, in a passage which may serve to introduce our topic, "To be universally intelligible is not the highest merit. A great mind cannot, without injurious constraint, shrink itself to the grasp of common passive readers." It is wrong therefore to expect it to sacrifice great qualities "that the multitude may keep pace with it."[1]

The situation which gave rise to Channing's complaint has grown measurably worse by our day, when the common passive reader determines the level of most publications. The mere pursuance of Milton's meaning requires an enforcement of attention, and the perception of his judgments requires an active sensibility incompatible with a state of relaxation. There is nothing in Milton for the reader who must be put at ease and treated only to the quickly apprehensible. But along with this turning away from the difficult, there is another cause at work, a feeling, quite truly grounded, that Milton's very arduousness of spirit calls for elevation on the part of the reader. Milton assumes an heroic stance, and he demands a similar stance of those who would meet him. An age which

1. "Remarks on the Character and Writings of John Milton," *The Works of William E. Channing, D.D.* (Boston, 1894), p. 503.

has come to suspect this as evidence of aristocratic tendency will then avoid Milton also for a moral reason, preferring, even when it agrees with him, to have the case stated in more plebeian fashion. Therefore the reading of Milton is more than a problem in communication; it is a problem also of gaining insight, or even of developing sympathy with the aristocratic intellectualism which breathes through all he wrote.

It can be shown that all of the features which make up Milton's arduous style proceed from three or four sources. The first of these is the primacy of the concept. What this primacy signifies is that in his prose Milton wrote primarily as a thinker and not as an artificer. That is to say, his units of composition are built upon concepts and not upon conventionalized expository patterns. For him the linguistic sentence was a means, to be expanded and shaped as the driving force of the thought required. Or perhaps it would be more meaningful to say that for him the sentence was an accommodation-form. He will put into it as much or as little as he needs, and often, as we shall see presently, he needed a great deal. This use of the sentence as an accommodation-form produces what is perhaps the most obvious feature of his style, the long period. What length must a sentence have to be called "long"? Of course our usual standard is the sentence we are accustomed to, and in present-day writing that sentence will run 20–30 words, to cite an average range for serious writing. Milton's sentences very frequently run 60–80 words, and many will exceed 100, the length of an average paragraph today.[2]

To examine Milton's method with the lengthy period, we

---

2. Some correlation appears to exist between the mentality of an era and the average length of sentence in use. The seventeenth century, the most introspective, philosophical, and "revolutionary" era of English history, wrote the longest sentence in English literature. The next era, broadly recognized as the eighteenth century, swung in the opposite direction, with a shorter and much more modelled or contrived sentence. The nineteenth century, again turned a little solemn and introspective, wrote a somewhat long and loose one. Now comes the twentieth century, with its journalism and its syncopated tempo, to write the shortest sentence of all.

may well begin with the second sentence of *Of Reformation in England,* an outstanding specimen of 373 words.

Sad it is to think how that doctrine of the gospel, planted by teachers divinely inspired, and by them winnowed and sifted from the chaff of overdated ceremonies, and refined to such a spiritual height and temper of purity, and knowledge of the Creator, that the body, with all the circumstances of time and place, were purified by the affections of the regenerate soul, and nothing left impure but sin; faith needing not the weak and fallible office of the senses, to be either the ushers or interpreters of heavenly mysteries, save where our Lord himself in his sacraments ordained; that such a doctrine should, through the grossness and blindness of her professors, and the fraud of deceivable traditions, drag so downwards, as to backslide into the Jewish beggary of old cast rudiments, and stumble forward another way into the new-vomited paganism of sensual idolatry, attributing purity or impurity to things indifferent, that they might bring the inward acts of the spirit to the outward and customary eye-service of the body, as if they could make God earthly and fleshly, because they could not make themselves heavenly and spiritual; they began to draw down all the divine intercourse between God and the soul, yea, the very shape of God himself, into an exterior and bodily form, urgently pretending a necessity and obligement of joining the body in a formal reverence, and worship circumscribed; they hallowed it, they fumed it, they sprinkled it, they bedecked it, not in robes of pure innocency, but of pure linen, with other deformed and fantastic dresses, in palls and mitres, gold and gewgaws fetched from Aaron's old wardrobe, or the flamins vestry: then was the priest set to con his motions and his postures, his liturgies and his lurries, till the soul by this means of overbodying herself, given up justly to fleshly delights, bated her wing apace downward: and finding the ease she had from her visible and sensuous colleague the body, in performance of religious duties, her pinions now broken, and flagging, shifted off from herself the labor of high soaring any more, forgot her heavenly flight, and left the dull and droiling carcase to plod in the old road, and drudging trade of outward conformity.[3]

---

3. *The Prose Works of John Milton,* ed. J. A. St. John (London, 1909–14), II, 364–65. Hereafter referred to as *Works.*

With reference to accommodation, let us attend to the scope of this sentence. It contains nothing less than a history of Christianity from the Protestant reformer's point of view. Four stages are given in this history: the early revelation of true Christianity; its later misinterpretation through the "grossness and blindness" of its followers; the growth of institutionalism; and finally the atrophy of true religion produced by undue attention to outward circumstance. It is, as we see, a complete narration, dressed out with many illuminating details. We shall discover that Milton habitually prolongs a sentence thus until it has covered the unit of its subject. He feels no compulsion to close the period out of regard for some established norm, since he has his eye on a different criterion of completeness. In line with the same practice, some of his sentences are so fitted that they contain complete arguments, or even an argument preceded by its expository narration. As an example of the sentence containing a unit of argument, we may note the following from *The Doctrine and Discipline of Divorce*.

And yet there follows upon this a worse temptation: for if he be such as hath spent his youth unblameably, and laid up his chiefest earthly comforts in the enjoyments of a contented marriage, nor did neglect that furtherance which was to be obtained therein by constant prayers; when he shall find himself bound fast to an uncomplying discord of nature, or, as it often happens, to an image of earth and phlegm, with whom he looked to be the copartner of a sweet and gladsome society, and sees withal that his bondage is now inevitable; though he be almost the strongest Christian, he will be ready to despair in virtue, and mutiny against Divine Providence; and this doubtless is the reason of those lapses, and that melancholy despair, which we see in many wedded persons, though they understand it not, or pretend other causes, because they know no remedy; and is of extreme danger: therefore when human frailty surcharged is at such a loss, charity ought to venture much, lest an overtossed faith endanger to shipwreck.[4]

---

4. *Works*, III, 194.

This sentence contains a complete hypothetical syllogism, which can be abstracted as follows:

> If the rigidity of the marriage relationship is not relaxed by charity, Christians will despair of finding their solace in that relationship.
> The rigidity of the marriage relationship is not at present relaxed by charity.
> Christians do despair of finding solace within that relationship (as shown by "those lapses and that melancholy despair, which we see in many wedded persons").

Thus the argument prescribes the content of the sentence and marshals it.

Let us look next at a specimen from the *Areopagitica* embodying not only the full syllogism but also a preparatory exposition.

> When a man writes to the world, he summons up all his reason and deliberation to assist him; he searches, meditates, is industrious, and likely consults and confers with his judicious friends; after all which done, he takes himself to be informed in what he writes, as well as any that writ before him; if in this most consummate act of his fidelity and ripeness, no years, no industry, no former proof of his abilities can bring him to that state of maturity, as not to be still mistrusted and suspected, unless he carry all his considerate diligence, all his midnight watchings, and expense of Palladian oil, to the hasty view of an unleisured licenser, perhaps much his younger, perhaps far his inferior in judgment, perhaps one who never knew the labor of bookwriting; and if he be not repulsed, or slighted, must appear in print like a puny with his guardian, and his censor's hand on the back of his title to be his bail and surety, that he is no idiot or seducer; it cannot be but a dishonor and derogation the author, to the book, to the privilege and dignity of learning.[5]

---

5. *Works*, II, 78–79.

In this utterance of 197 words, every detail pertains to the one concept of the responsibility and dignity of learning; yet closer inspection reveals that a two-part structure is accommodated. First there is the "narration," a regular part of the classical oration, here setting forth the industry and conscientiousness of authors. This is followed by a hypothetical argument saying, in effect, that if all these guarantees of sober and honest performance are not enough to entitle authors to liberty, there can be no respect for learning or learned men in the commonwealth. Thus the sentence is prolonged, one might say, until the speech is made, and the speech is not a series of loosely related assertions but a structure defined by standard principles of logic and rhetoric.

Apart from mere length, which as Whatley and other writers on style observe, imposes a burden upon the memory too great to be expected of everyone, there is in the longer Miltonic sentence the additional tax of complexity. Of course Milton was somewhat influenced by Latin grammar, but here we are less interested in measuring literary influences than in analyzing the reading problem which he presents in our day. That problem is created largely by his intricate elaboration within the long period. For an especially apt illustration of this I should like to return to *Of Reformation in England* and follow the sentence which introduces that work.

Amidst those deep and retired thoughts, which, with every man Christianly instructed, ought to be most frequent, of God and of his miraculous ways and works among men, and of our religion and works, to be performed to him; after the story of our Saviour Christ, suffering to the lowest bent of weakness in the flesh, and presently triumphing to the highest pitch of glory in the spirit, which drew up his body also; till we in both be united to him in the revelation of his kingdom, I do not know of anything more worthy to take up the whole passion of pity on the one side, and joy on the other, than to consider first the foul and sudden corruption, and then, after many a tedious age, the long deferred, but much more wonderful and happy reformation of the church in these latter days.[6]

It will be agreed, I feel, that the following features require a more than ordinary effort of attention and memory: 1) The rhetorical interruptions, whereby *which* is separated from its verb *ought to be,* and *thoughts* is separated from its prepositional modifier *of God and of his miraculous works and ways among men.*—2) The progressive particularization of *our Saviour Christ,* wherein the substantive is modified by two participial constructions, *suffering to the lowest bent of weakness in the flesh* and *triumphing to the highest pitch of glory in the spirit;* wherein again the substantive *spirit* takes a modifier in the clause *which drew up his body also,* and the verb *drew up* of the clause is qualified by the adverbial clause *till we in both be united to him in the revelation of his kingdom.* This is a type of elaboration in which, as the account unfolds, each detail seems to require a gloss, which is offered in a construction of some weight or length.—3) The extensive parallelism of the last part, beginning with *the whole passion of pity on the one side.*—4) The suspended structure which withholds the topic phrase of the tract, *happy reformation of the church,* until almost the end of the sentence.

All of these qualities of length, scope, and complexity made the Miltonic sentence a formidable construction, and we are curious to know why he was able to use it with public success. The first circumstance we must take into account is that he lived in a tough-minded period of Western culture. It was a time when the foundations of the state were being searched out; when the relationship between religion and political authority was being re-defined, to the disregard of old customs; and when sermons were powerful arguments, beginning with first principles and moving down through a long chain of deductions. It was a time in which every thinking man vir-

6. *Works,* II, 364.

tually had to be either a revolutionary or a counter-revolutionary; and there is something in such intellectual climate which scorns prettification and mincing measure. The public therefore met Milton's impassioned interest with an equal passion. But by public we do not mean here the half-educated masses of today; Milton's public was rather a sternly educated minority, which had been taught to recognize an argument when it saw one, and even to analyze its source.

Further evidence of the absorbing interest in the argumentative burden of prose expression may be seen in the way he employs the extended metaphor. Milton grew up in the age of the metaphysical conceit. We now understand that for Elizabethans and Jacobeans a metaphor went far beyond mere ornamentation to enter into the very heart of a predication. Rosemund Tuve in particular has shown that for the poets of the period an image was an argument, so understood and so used.[7] We would hardly expect it to be any less so in prose. When Milton brings in a metaphor, he makes full use of its probative value, and this involved, along with confidence in the architectonic power of the image, a belief that it affirmed something about the case in point. Thus the metaphor was not idle or decorative merely, and it dominated the passage to the eclipse of sentence units. This will explain why, when Milton begins a metaphor, he will scarcely abandon it until the last appropriate application has been made and the similitude established beyond reasonable question.

The *Areopagitica* teems with brilliant extended figures, of which two will be cited. Here is an image of truth, carried through three sentences.

Truth indeed came once into the world with her divine master, and was a perfect shape most glorious to look on: but when he had ascended, and his apostles after him were laid asleep, then straight arose a wicked race of deceivers, who, as that story goes of the Egyptian Typhon with his conspirators, how they dealt with

7. See her *Elizabethan and Metaphysical Imagery* (Chicago, 1947), pp. 284–99.

the good Osiris, took the virgin Truth, hewed her lovely form into a thousand pieces, and scattered them to the four winds. From that time ever since, the sad friends of Truth, such as durst appear, imitating the careful search that Isis made after the body of Osiris, went up and down gathering limb by limb still as they could find them. We have not found them all, lords and commons, nor ever shall do, till her master's second coming; he shall bring together every joint and member, and shall mold them into an immortal feature of loveliness and perfection. Suffer not these licensing prohibitions to stand at every place of opportunity forbidding and disturbing them that continue seeking, that continue to do our obsequies to the torn body of our martyred saint.[8]

And here is Milton's defense of the intellectually free community, rendered in a military metaphor.

First, when a city shall be as it were besieged and blocked about, her navigable river infested, inroads and incursions round, defiance and battle oft rumored to be marching up, even to her walls and suburb trenches; that then the people, or the greater part, more than at other times, wholly taken up with the study of highest and most important matters to be reformed, should be disputing, reasoning, reading, inventing, discoursing, even to a rarity and admiration, things not before discoursed or written of, argues first a singular good will, contentedness, and confidence in your prudent foresight, and safe government, lords and commons; and from thence derives itself to a gallant bravery and well grounded contempt of their enemies, as if there were no small number of as great spirits among us, as was his who, when Rome was nigh besieged by Hannibal, being in the city, bought that piece of ground at no cheap rate, whereupon Hannibal himself encamped his own regiment.[9]

Milton's concept of church government according to Scripture is thus presented in *The Reason of Church Government Urged Against Prelaty:*

8. *Works*, II, 89.
9. *Works*, II, 93–94.

Did God take such delight in measuring out the pillars, arches, and doors of a material temple? Was he so punctual and circumspect in lavers, altars and sacrifices soon after to be abrogated, lest any of these should have been made contrary to his mind? Is not a far more perfect work, more agreeable to his perfections, in the most perfect state of the church militant, the new alliance to God to man? Should not he rather now by his own prescribed discipline have cast his line and level upon the soul of man, which is his rational temple, and, by the divine square and compass thereof, form and regenerate in us the lovely shapes of virtues and graces, the sooner to edify and accomplish that immortal stature of Christ's body, which is his church, in all her glorious lineaments and proportions?[10]

What we are especially called upon to note in these examples is the boldness of figuration, by which the concept survives the pressure of many, and sometimes rather concrete, tests of correspondence, as the analogy enlarges. The author's faith in the figure as an organizing principle is likely evidence that he sees the world as form, the more of which can be drawn out the better. To a later day, any figure carried beyond modest length runs the danger of turning into an ironic commentary upon its analogue, but to Milton, as to the seventeenth century generally, it was a window to look through. Now quite literally the conceit is a concept, and we have found it to be another organizing medium of this intellectual prose, and a second proof that some texture of thought precedes the mere linguistic expression, and holds itself superior to it.

While the primacy of the concept is responsible for these formal features of style, we must look elsewhere for the source of its vigor. Certainly another reason that Milton is a taxing author to read is the restless energy that permeates his substance. He never allows the reader to remain inert, and this is because there were few things toward which Milton himself was indifferent. One revelation of the active mind is the zeal and completeness with which it sorts things according to some

10. *Works*, II, 446.

scale of values; and judged by that standard Milton's mind is active in the extreme. To approach this a little more systematically, what one discovers with one's first reading of the prose is that Milton is constantly attentive to the degrees of things, and his range of valuations, extending from those things which can be described only through his elegant curses to those which require the language of religious or poetic eulogy, is very great. Indeed, "things indifferent," to employ a phrase used by Milton himself, play a very small part in his writing, which rather tends to be juridical in the highest measure. And the vitality contributed by this awareness of difference he increased by widening the gulf between the bad and the good. These contrarieties are managed in various ways: sometimes they are made up of single nouns of opposed meaning; sometimes of other parts of speech or of phrases; but always it would take a dull reader to miss the opposed valuations. A sentence from *The Doctrine and Discipline of Divorce* will afford some good examples.

Hence it is, that error supports custom, custom countenances error: and these two between them would persecute and chase away all truth and solid wisdom out of human life, were it not that God, rather than man, once in many ages calls together the prudent and religious counsels of men, deputed to repress the encroachments, and to work off the inveterate blots and obscurities wrought upon our minds by the subtle insinuating of error and custom; who, with the numerous and vulgar train of their followers, make it their chief design to envy and cry down the industry of free reasoning, under the terms of humor and innovation; as if the womb of teeming truth were to be closed up, if she presume to bring forth aught that sorts not with their unchewed notions and suppositions.[11]

The vigor of this passage arises from a continuing series of contrasts, comprising the following: *error and custom* with *truth and solid wisdom; God* with *man; prudent and religious*

----

11. *Works*, III, 172.

counsels with *encroachments* and also with *inveterate blots and obscurities; subtle insinuating of error and custom* with *industry of free reasoning;* and *womb of teeming truth* with *unchewed notions and suppositions.*

Here is another passage, from *Of Reformation in England.*

So that in this manner the prelates, both then and ever since, coming from a mean and plebeian life on a sudden to be lords of stately palaces, rich furniture, delicious fare, and princely attendance, thought the plain and homespun verity of Christ's gospel unfit any longer to hold their lordships' acquaintance, unless the poor threadbare matron were put into better clothes; her chaste and modest vail, surrounded with celestial beams, they overlaid with wanton tresses, and in a staring tire bespeckled her with all the gaudy allurements of a whore.[12]

In this the clash is between *plebeian life* and *stately palaces, rich furniture,* etc.; *homespun verity* and *lordship's acquaintance; threadbare matron* and *better clothes; chaste and modest vail* and *wanton tresses, staring tire,* and *gaudy allurements of a whore.* Lastly I should like to take a sentence from the same work, which has been admired by Aldous Huxley for its energy.

Thus then did the spirit of unity and meekness inspire and animate every joint and sinew of the mystical body; but now the gravest and worthiest minister, a true bishop of his fold, shall be reviled and ruffled by an insulting and only canon-wise prelate, as if he were some slight paltry companion: and the people of God, redeemed and washed with Christ's blood, and dignified with so many glorious titles of saints and sons in the gospel, are now no better reputed than impure ethnics and lay dogs; stones, pillars, and crucifixes, have now the honour and the alms due to Christ's living members; the table of communion, now become a table of separation, stands like an exalted platform on the brow of the quire, fortified with bulwark and barricado, to keep off the profane

12. *Works,* II, 382.

touch of the laics, whilst the obscene and surfeited priest scruples not to paw and mammock the sacramental bread as familiarly as his tavern biscuit.[13]

In this typical specimen of Milton's vehemence, *gravest and worthiest minister, a true bishop* contrasts with *insulting and only canon-wise prelate* and with *slight paltry companion; the people of God, redeemed and washed with Christ's blood, and dignified with so many glorious titles of saints and sons in the gospel* with *impure ethnics* and *lay dogs; stones, pillars, and crucifixes* with *Christ's living members; communion* with *separation; fortified with bulwark and barricado* with the earlier *unity and meekness; obscene, surfeited, paw,* and *mammock* with *priest;* and *sacramental bread* with *tavern biscuit.*

The effect of such sustained contrast is to produce a high degree of tonicity, and here in a word is why Milton's prose seems never relaxed. His pervading consciousness of the combat of good and evil caused him to engage in constant projections of that combat. In a manner of speaking, Milton always writes from a "prejudice," which proves to be on inspection his conviction as a Christian and as a political and moral preacher, that, as the good has been judged, the duty of a publicist is to show it separated with the utmost clearness of distinction from the bad. Accordingly Milton's expositions, if one follows them intently, cause one to accept one thing and reprobate another unceasingly.

In consequence there appears in many passages a quality of style which I shall call the superlative mode. His very reaching out toward the two extremes of a gauge of value drives him to couch expression in terms raised to their highest degree. Often we see this in the superlative form of the adjective. But we see it also in his employment of words which even in their grammatically positive forms have acquired a kind of superlative sense. Finally we see it on occasion in a

---

13. *Works*, II, 377–78.

pattern of incremental repetition which he uses to impress us with his most impassioned thoughts. The wonderful closing prayer from *Of Reformation in England* contains examples of all of these superlatives. Here are the closing paragraphs.

And now we know, O thou our most certain hope and defence, that thine enemies have been consulting all the sorceries of the great whore, and have joined their plots with that sad intelligencing tyrant that mischiefs the world with his mines of Ophir, and lies thirsting to revenge his naval ruins that have larded our seas: but let them all take counsel together, and let it come to nought; let them decree, and do thou cancel it; let them gather themselves, and be scattered; let them embattle themselves, and be broken, for thou art with us.

Then, amidst the hymns and hallelujahs of saints, some one may perhaps be heard offering at high strains in new and lofty measures, to sing and celebrate thy divine mercies and marvellous judgments in this land throughout all ages; whereby this great and warlike nation, instructed and inured to the fervent and continual practice of truth and righteousness, and casting far from her the rags of her old vices, may press on hard to that high and happy emulation to be found the soberest, wisest, and most Christian people at that day, when thou, the eternal and shortly-expected King, shalt open the clouds to judge the several kingdoms of the world, and distributing national honours and rewards to religious and just commonwealths, shalt put an end to all earthly tyrannies, proclaiming thy universal and mild monarchy through heaven and earth; where they undoubtedly, that by their labors, counsels and prayers, have been earnest for the common good of religion and their country, shall receive above the inferior orders of the blessed, the regal addition of principalities, legions, and thrones into their glorious titles, and in supereminence of beatific vision, progressing the dateless and irrevoluble circle of eternity, shall clasp inseparable hands with joy and bliss, in overmeasure, for ever.

But they contrary, that by the impairing and diminution of the true faith, the distresses and servitude of their country, aspire to high dignity, rule, and promotion here, after a shameful end in this life (which God grant them), shall be thrown down eternally into the darkest and deepest gulf of hell, where under the despiteful control, the trample and spurn of all the other damned, that in the anguish of their torture, shall have no other ease than to exercise a raving and bestial tyranny over them as their slaves and negroes, they shall remain in that plight for ever, the basest, the lowermost, the most dejected, most underfoot, and downtrodden vassals of perdition.[14]

Let us mark the bristling superlatives. Of adjectives in superlative form we find *most certain, soberest, wisest, most Christian, darkest, deepest, basest, lowermost, most dejected, most underfoot,* and [*most*] *downtrodden.* Of those words which have a superlative force or meaning, I would list—allowing that this must be a matter of judgment—*naught, cancel, broken, marvellous, fervent, eternal, universal, undoubtedly, supereminence, beatific, dateless, irrevoluble, eternity, inseparable, overmeasure, for ever,* and *eternally.* But the most interesting form of the superlative mode is the pattern of repetition by which Milton, through a progressive accumulation of substantives and adjectives, builds up a crescendo. First there will be one or more groups of two, then perhaps a group of three, and finally, for the supreme effect, a breathtaking collocation of five. Such a pattern appears in the concluding sentence of the prayer: *impairing* and *diminution; distresses* and *servitude; dignity, rule,* and *promotion; darkest* and *deepest; control, trample,* and *spurn; raving* and *bestial; slaves* and *negroes; basest, lowermost, most dejected, most underfoot and downtrodden.* Here, it will be noticed, the sequence is 2-2-3-2-3-2-2-5. The pattern in itself is revealing. First there are two pairs which ready us for attaining the group of three; then another pair to rest upon before we attain the group of three again; then two more pairs for a longer respite while we ready ourselves for the supreme effort of the group of five.

The prayer is not, of course, an ordinary passage; yet what is seen here is discoverable in some measure in all of Milton's

---

14. *Works*, II, 418-19.

prose. He wrote in this superlative vein because his principal aim was the divorcement of good and evil. To show these wide apart, he had to talk in terms of best and worst, and being a rhetorician of vast resources, he found ways of making the superlative even more eminent than our regular grammatical forms make it, which naturally marks him as a great creative user of the language.

The topic of grouping appropriately introduces another aspect of Milton's style which I shall refer to more specifically as systematic collocation. No one can read him with the object of forming some descriptive image of his prose without being impressed by his frequent use of pairs of words similar in meaning to express a single object or idea. These pairs will be comprised, in a roughly equal number of instances, of nouns and of adjectives, though fairly often two verbs will make up the collocation and occasionally two adverbs. It seems probable that these pairs, more than any other single feature of the style, give the impression of thickness, which is in turn the source of the impression of strength. Or to present this in another way, what the pairs create is the effect of dimension. It needs no proving at this stage that Milton had too well stored a mind and too genuine a passion to coast along on mere fluency. If he used two words where another author would use one, that fact affords presumption that his second word had its margin of meaningful addition to contribute. And so we find it: these pairs of substantives give his prose a dimensional quality, because this one will show one aspect of the thing named and that one another. It would require a rather long list to include the variety of aspects which Milton will bring out by his practice of double naming; sometimes it is in form and substance, or the conceptual and the material nature of the thing; sometimes it is appearance and meaning; sometimes process and tendency; sometimes one modifier will express the active and another the passive nature of the thing described. Always the practice causes his subject matter to convey this sensation of depth and realness, which is a principal factor in the vitality of his style.

We shall look at some examples of this highly interesting method. The first is from the *Areopagitica*. I have italicized the pairs.

Methinks I see in my mind a *noble* and *puissant* nation rousing herself like a strong man after a sleep, and shaking her invincible locks: methinks I see her as an eagle mewing her mighty youth, and kindling her undazzled eyes at the full midday beam, *purging* and *unscaling* her long abused sight at the fountain itself of heavenly radiance; while the whole noise of *timorous* and *flocking* birds, with those also that love the twilight, flutter about, amazed at what she means, and in their envious gabble, would prognosticate a year of *sects* and *schisms*.[15]

Noble and *puissant* direct attention to ethical and to physical attributes; *purging* and *scaling* do not form so complementary a pair but perhaps denote two distinct phases of a process; *timorous* and *flocking* is an excellent pair to show inward nature and outward behavior, and must be accounted one of the most successful uses of the method; *sects* and *schisms* would seem to refer to social or ecclesiastical and to theological aspects of division.

In a sentence from *Of Reformation in England*, he says: "But what do I stand reckoning upon *advantages* and *gains* lost by the *misrule* and *turbulency* of the prelates?[16] *Advantages* and *gains* stand for two sorts of progress made prior to the *misrule* and *turbulency* of the prelates, which in turn signify the formal outward policies and the inner spirit of ambition and presumption. From the *Doctrine and Discipline of Divorce:* "The *ignorance* and *mistake* of this high point hath heaped up one huge half of all the misery that hath been since Adam."[17] Here *ignorance* would seem to describe a passive lack of awareness, whereas *mistake* describes active misapprehension or misapplication. Finally here are examples from

15. *Works*, II, 94.
16. *Works*, II, 401.
17. *Works*, III, 175.

Animadversions upon the Remonstrant's Defence Against Smectymnuus.

We all know that in *private* or *personal* injuries, yea, in public sufferings for the cause of Christ, his *rule* and *example* teaches us to be so far from a readiness to speak evil, as not to answer the reviler in his language, though never so much provoked: yet in the *detecting* and *convincing* of any notorious enemy to *truth* and his *country's peace*, especially that is conceited to have a *voluble* and *smart* fluence of tongue, and in the vain confidence of that, and out of a more tenacious cling to worldly respects, stands up for all the rest to justify a *long usurpation* and *convicted pseudepiscopy* of prelates, with all their ceremonies, liturgies and tyrannies, which *God* and *man* are now ready to *explode* and *hiss out of the land:* I suppose, and more than suppose, it will be nothing disagreeing from Christian meekness to handle such a one in a rougher accent, and to send home his haughtiness well besputed with his own holy water.[18]

Here *private* and *personal* may be taken as giving us two aspects of the individual; *rule* and *example* differ as abstract and concrete; *detecting* and *convincing* (the latter apparently in the older sense of "overcoming") denote two stages of a process; *truth* and *his country's peace* may be taken to express the metaphysical and the embodied forms of the same thing; *voluble* and *smart* seem to refer to what is perceivable by the senses and by the intellect respectively; *long usurpation* and *convicted pseudepiscopy* differ as simple action and action which has been judged: *God* and *man* bring together the divine and the human; *explode* and *hiss out of the land* again express two stages of a process.

In the manner here indicated, these collocations serve to give the style a wonderful richness of thought. The reader feels that he is being shown both the *esse* and the *potesse* of the object named. At least, he gets a look at its manifold nature.

---

18. *Works*, III, 42–43.

The way in which Milton fills out the subject for his reader is at once lavish and perspicuous. Just as his figures were seen to have a prolonged correspondence, beyond what the casual or unthinking writer would bring to view, so his substantives and predicates are assembled upon a principle of penetration or depth of description.

Our general impression of Milton—an impression we get in some degree of all the great writers of his period and of the Elizabethan period before it—is that his thought dominates the medium. While the distinction between what is said and the form of saying it can never be drawn absolutely, it is yet to be remarked that some writers seem to compose with an awareness of how their matter will look upon the page, or how it will sound in the parlor; others seem to keep their main attention upon currently preferred terms and idioms. Again, some writers seem to accept the risk of suspension, transposition, and involution out of conscious elegance; Milton seems rather to require them out of strength of purpose. He was not a writer of writing, but consistently a writer of substance, and the language was his instrumentality, which he used with the familiar boldness of a master. One would go far to find a better illustration of the saying of John Peale Bishop that the English language is like a woman; it is most likely to yield after one has shown it a little violence. All of the great prose writers of the Elizabethan age and the Seventeenth century were perfectly capable of showing it that violence, and I believe this is the true reason that a lover of eloquence today reads their works with irrepressible admiration. The tremendous suspensions and ramifications they were willing to create; their readiness to make function the test of grammar and to coin according to need, through all of which a rational, though not always a formal or codified syntax survives—these things bespeak a sort of magisterial attitude toward language which has been lost in the intervening centuries.

It is quite possible that long years of accumulated usage tend to act as a deterrent to a free and imaginative use of language. So many stereotypes have had time to form themselves, and so many manuals of usage have been issued that the choice would seem to lie between simple compliance and open rebellion. Either one uses the language as the leaders of one's social and business world use it, or one makes a decisive break and uses it in open defiance of the conventionalized patterns. We may remember in this connection that when the new movement in modern literature got underway in the second decade of this century, its leaders proved themselves the most defiant and brash kind of rebels as they embarked upon the work of resuscitation and refurbishment, and it was to the Elizabethans especially that they looked for sanction and guidance. But the rebel with this program faces a dilemma: he cannot infuse life into the old forms that he knows are depriving expression of all vitality, and he exhausts himself in the campaign to smash and get rid of them.

That is partly an historical observation, and our interest is in laying bare the movement of a great eloquence. Yet if we had to answer whether some heroic style like that of Milton cannot be formed for our own day, when millions might rejoice to hear a sonorous voice speaking out of a deep learning in our traditions, our answer would surely be, yes. And if asked how, we would begin our counsel by telling the writer to heed the advice in Emerson's *American Scholar*—better indeed than Emerson heeded it himself—to look upon himself not as a writer but as a man writing, and to try to live in that character. As long as one does that, it is most likely that the concept will dominate the medium, and that one will use, with inventive freedom, such conventionality as is necessary to language. A timid correctness, like perfect lucidity, sometimes shows that more attention has been devoted to the form than to the thought, and this may give the writing a kind of hard surface which impedes sympathy between writer and reader. Finally, one should remember that people like to feel they are hearing of the solid fact and substance of the world, and those epithets which give us glimpses of its concreteness and contingency are the best guarantors of that. The regular balancing of abstract and concrete modifiers, which we meet regularly in Shakespeare, mirrors, indeed, the situation all of us face in daily living, where general principles are clear in theory but are conditioned in their application to the concrete world. The man of eloquence must be a lover of "the world's body" to the extent of being able to give it a fond description.

With these conditions practically realized, we might again have orators of the heroic mold. But the change would have to include the public also, for, on a second thought suggested by Whitman, to have great orators there must be great audiences too.

Chapter VII

THE SPACIOUSNESS
OF OLD RHETORIC

F EW SPECIES of composition seem so antiquated, so little available for any practical purpose today, as the oratory in which the generation of our grandparents delighted. The type of discourse which they would ride miles in wagons to hear, or would regard as the special treat of some festive occasion, fills most people today with an acute sense of discomfort. Somehow, it makes them embarrassed. They become conscious of themselves, conscious of pretensions in it, and they think it well consigned to the museum. But its very ability to inspire antipathy, as distinguished from indifference, suggests the presence of something interesting.

The student of rhetoric should accordingly sense here the chance for a discovery, and as he begins to listen for its revealing quality, the first thing he becomes aware of is a "spaciousness." This is, of course, a broad impression, which requires its own analysis. As we listen more carefully, then, it seems that between the speech itself and the things it is meant to signify, something stands—perhaps it is only an empty space —but something is there to prevent immediate realizations and references. For an experience of the sensation, let us for a moment go back to 1850 and attune our ears to an address by Representative Andrew Ewing, on the subject of the sale of the public lands.

We have afforded a refuge to the down-trodden nations of the Old World, and organized system of internal improvement and public education, which have no parallel in the history of mankind. Why should we not continue and enlarge the system which has so much contributed to these results? If our Pacific Coast should be lined with its hundred cities, extending from the northern boundary of Oregon down to San Diego; if the vast interior hills and valleys could be filled with lowing herds and fruitful fields of a thriving and industrious people; and if the busy hum of ten thousand work-shops could be daily heard over the placid waters of the Pacific, would our government be poorer or our country less able to meet her obligations than at present?[1]

Despite the allusions to geographical localities, does not the speaker seem to be speaking *in vacuo?* His words do not im-pinge upon a circumambient reality; his concepts seem not to have definite correspondences, but to be general, and as it were, mobile. "Spread-eagle" and "high-flown" are two modi-fiers with which people have sought to catch the quality of such speech.

In this work we are interested both in causes and the moral quality of causes, and when an orator appears to speak of sub-jects without an immediate apperception of them, we become curious about the kind of world he is living in. Was this type of orator sick, as some have inferred? Was he suffering from some kind of auto-intoxication which produces insulation from reality? Charles Egbert Craddock in her novel *Where the Battle Was Fought* has left a satirical picture of the type. Its personification is General Vayne, who holds everything up to a "moral magnifying glass." "Through this unique lens life loomed up as a rather large affair. In the rickety courthouse in the village of Chattalla, five miles out there to the south, Gen-eral Vayne beheld a temple of justice. He translated an office-holder as the sworn servant of the people. The State was this great commonwealth, and its seal a proud escutcheon. A fall in cotton struck him as a blow to the commerce of the world.

---

1. *The Congressional Globe,* Thirty-first Congress, First Session (June 21, 1850), p. 1250.

From an adverse political fortune he augured the swift ruin of
the country."² There is the possibility that this type was sick
with a kind of vanity and egocentricity, and that has frequently been offered as a diagnosis. But on the other hand, there is
the possibility that such men were larger than we, with our
petty and contentious style, and because larger more exposed
in those limitations which they had. The heroes in tragedies
also talk bigger than life. Perhaps the source of our discomfort
is that this kind of speech comes to us as an admonition that
there were giants in the earth before us, mighty men, men of
renown. But before we are ready for any conclusion, we must
isolate the cause of our intimation.

As we scan the old oratory for the chief offender against
modern sensibility, we are certain to rank in high position, if
not first, *the uncontested term.* By this we mean the term
which seems to invite a contest, but which apparently is not
so regarded in its own context. Most of these are terms which
scandalize the modern reader with their generality, so that he
wonders how the speaker ever took the risk of using them.
No experienced speaker interlards his discourse with terms
which are themselves controversial. He may build his case on
one or two such terms, after giving them *ad hoc* definitions,
but to multiply them is to create a force of resistance which
almost no speech can overcome. Yet in this period we have
speeches which seem made up almost from beginning to end
of phrases loose in scope and but weakly defensible. Yet the
old orator who employed these terms of sweeping generality
knew something of his audience's state of mind and was confident of his effect. And the public generally responded by
putting him in the genus "great man." This brings us to the
rhetorical situation, which must be described in some detail.

We have said that this orator of the old-fashioned mold, who
is using the uncontested term, passes on his collection of gen-

---

2. *Where the Battle Was Fought* (Boston and New York, 1900),
p. 4.

eralities in full expectation that they will be received as legal tender. He is taking a very advanced position, which could be undermined easily, were the will to do so present. But the will was not present, and this is the most significant fact in our explanation. The orator had, in any typical audience, not only a previously indoctrinated group, but a group of quite similar indoctrination. Of course, we are using such phrases for purposes of comparison with today. It is now a truism that the homogeneity of belief which obtained three generations ago has largely disappeared. Such belief was, in a manner of conceiving it, the old orator's capital. And it was, if we may trust the figure further, an initial asset which made further operations possible.

If we knew how this capital is accumulated, we would possess one of the secrets of civilization. All we know is that whatever spells the essential unity of a people in belief and attachment contains the answer. The best we can do at this stage is look into the mechanism of relationship between this level of generality and the effectiveness of a speech.

We must keep in mind that "general" is itself a relative modifier, and that the degree of generality with which one may express one's thoughts is very wide. One may refer, for example, to a certain event as a *murder*, a *crime*, an *act*, or an *occurrence*. We assume that none of these terms is inherently falsifying, because none of them is in any prior sense required. Levels of generality do not contradict one another; they supplement one another by bringing out different foci of interest. Every level of generality has its uses: the Bible can tell the story of creation in a few hundred words, and it is doubtless well that it should be told there in that way. Let us therefore take a guarded position here and claim only that one's level of generality tells something of one's approach to a subject. We shall find certain refinements of application possible as we go on.

With this as a starting point, we should be prepared for a more intensive look at the diction of the old school. For pur-

poses of this analysis I shall choose something that is historically obscure. Great occasions sometimes deflect our judgment
by their special circumstances. The passage below is from a
speech made by the Honorable Charles J. Faulkner at an agricultural fair in Virginia in 1858. Both speaker and event have
passed into relative oblivion, and we can therefore view this
as a fairly stock specimen of the oratory in vogue a hundred
years ago to grace local celebrations. Let us attend to it carefully for its references.

If we look to the past or to the present we shall find that the
permanent power of any nation has always been in proportion to its
cultivation of the soil—those republics which during the earlier
and middle ages, were indebted for their growth mainly to commerce, did for a moment, indeed, cast a dazzling splendor across
the pathway of time; but they soon passed from among the powers
of the earth, leaving behind them not a memorial of their proud
and ephemeral destiny whilst other nations, which looked to the
products of the soil for the elements of their strength, found in each
successive year the unfailing sources of national aggrandizement
and power. Of all the nations of antiquity, the Romans were most
persistently devoted to agriculture, and many of the maxims taught
by their experience, and transmitted to us by their distinguished
writers, are not unworthy, even at this time, of the notice of the
intelligent farmers of this valley. It was in their schools of country
life—a *vita rustica*—as their own great orator informs us, that they
imbibed those noble sentiments which rendered the Roman name
more illustrious than all their famous victories, and there, that
they acquired those habits of labor, frugality, justice and that high
standard of moral virtue which made them the easy masters of
their race.[3]

A modern mind trained in the habit of analysis will be horri-
fied by the number of large and unexamined phrases passing

---

3. *Address Delivered by Hon. Charles J. Faulkner before the Valley
Agricultural Society of Virginia, at their Fair Grounds near Winchester,
October 21, 1858* (Washington, 1858), pp. 3-4.

by in even this brief excerpt. "Permanent power of any nation"; "earlier and middle ages"; "cast a dazzling splendor across the pathway of time"; "proud and ephemeral destiny"; "noble sentiments which rendered the Roman name more illustrious"; and "high standards of moral virtue" are but a selection. Comparatively speaking, the tone of this oration is fairly subdued, but it is in the grand style, and these phrases are the medium. With this passage before us for reference, I wish to discuss one matter of effect, and one of cause or enabling condition.

It will be quickly perceived that the phrases in question have resonances, both historical and literary, and that this resonance is what we have been calling spaciousness. Instead of the single note (prized for purposes of analysis) they are widths of sound and meaning; they tend to echo over broad areas and to call up generalized associations. This resonance is the interstice between what is said and the thing signified. In this way then the generality of the phrase may be definitely linked with an effect.

But the second question is our principal interest: how was the orator able to use them with full public consent when he cannot do so today?

I am going to suggest that the orator then enjoyed a privilege which can be compared to the lawyer's "right of assumption." This is the right to assume that precedents are valid, that forms will persist, and that in general one may build today on what was created yesterday. What mankind has sanctified with usage has a presumption in its favor. Such presumption, it was felt, instead of being an obstacle to progress, furnishes the ground for progress. More simply, yesterday's achievements are also contributions to progress. It is he who insists upon beginning every day *de novo* who denies the reality of progress. Accordingly, consider the American orator in the intellectual climate of this time. He was comfortably circumstanced with reference to things he could "know" and presume everyone else to know in the same way. Freedom and morality were constants; the Constitution was the codification of all that was politically feasible; Christianity of all that was morally authorized. Rome stood as an exemplum of what may happen to nations; the American and French Revolutions had taught rulers their necessary limitations. Civilization has thought over its thousands of years of history and has made some generalizations which are the premises of other arguments but which are not issues themselves. When one asserts that the Romans had a "high standard of moral virtue which made them the easy masters of their race," one is affirming a doctrine of causality in a sweeping way. If one had to stop and "prove" that moral virtue makes one master, one obviously would have to start farther down the ladder of assumption. But these things were not in the area of argument because progress was positive and that meant that some things have to be assimilated as truths. Men were not condemned to repeat history, because they remembered its lessons. To the extent that the mind had made its summations, it was free to go forward, and forward meant in the direction of more inclusive conceptions. The orator who pauses along the way to argue a point which no one challenges only demeans the occasion. Therefore the orator of the period we have defined did not feel that he had to argue the significance of everything to which he attached significance. Some things were fixed by universal enlightened consensus; and they could be used as steps for getting at matters which were less settled and hence were proper subjects for deliberation. Deliberation is good only because it decreases the number of things it is necessary to deliberate about.

Consequently when we wonder how he could use such expressions without trace of compunction, we forget that the expressions did not need apology. The speaker of the present who used like terms would, on the contrary, meet a contest at every step of the way. His audience would not swallow such clusters of related meanings. But at that time a number of unities, including the unity of past and present, the unity of moral sets and of causal sets, furnished the ground for discourse in "uncontested terms." Only such substratum of agreement makes possible the panoramic treatment.

We can infer important conclusions about a civilization when we know that its debates and controversies occur at outpost positions rather than within the citadel itself. If these occur at a very elementary level, we suspect that the culture has not defined itself, or that it is decayed and threatened with dissolution. Where the chief subject of debate is the relative validity of Homoiousianism and Homoousianism, or the conventions of courtly love, we feel confident that a great deal has been cached away in the form of settled conclusions, and that such shaking as proceeds from controversies of this kind, although they may agitate the superstructure, will hardly be felt as far down as the foundations. I would say the same is suggested by the great American debate over whether the Constitution was a "constitution" or a "compact," despite its unfortunate sequel.

At this stage of cultural development the commonplaces of opinion and conduct form a sort of *textus receptus,* and the emendations are confined to minor matters. Conversely, when the disagreement is over extremely elementary matters, survival itself may be at stake. It seems to me that modern debates over the validity of the law of contradiction may be a disagreement of this kind. The soundness of a culture may well be measured by this ability to recognize what is extraneous. One knows what to do with the extraneous, even if one decides upon a policy of temporary accommodation. It is when the line dividing us from the extraneous begins to fade that we are assailed with destructive doubts. Disagreements over the most fundamental subjects leave us puzzled as to "where we are" if not as to "what we are." The speaker whom we have been characterizing felt sure of the demarcation. That gave him his freedom, and was the source of his simplicity.

When we reflect further that the old oratory had a certain judicial flavor about it, we are prompted to ask whether thinking as then conceived did not have a different status from today's thinking. One is led to make this query by the suggestion that when the most fundamental propositions of a culture are under attack, then it becomes a duty to "think for one's self." Not that it is a bad thing to think; yet when the whole emphasis is upon "thinking for one's self," it is hard to avoid a feeling that certain postulates have broken down, and the most courage we can muster is to ask people, not to "think in a certain direction," but to "think for themselves." Where the primary directive of thinking is known, the object of thinking will not be mere cerebral motion (as some exponents of the policy of thinking for one's self leave us to infer), but rather the object of such thinking, or knowledge. This is a very rudimentary proposition, but it deserves attention because the modern tendency has reversed a previous order. From the position that only propositions are interesting because they alone make judgments, we are passing to a position in which only evidence is interesting because it alone is uncontaminated by propositions. In brief, interest has shifted from inference to reportage, and this has had a demonstrable effect upon the tone of oratory. The large resonant phrase is itself a kind of condensed proposition; as propositions begin to sink with the general sagging of the substructure, the phrases must do the same. Obviously we are pointing here to a profound cultural change, and the same shifts can be seen in literature; the poet or novelist may feel that the content of his consciousness is more valid (and this will be true even of those who have not formulated the belief) than the formal arrangement which would be produced by selection, abstraction, and arrangement. Or viewed in another respect, experiential order has taken precedence over logical order.

The object of an oration made on the conditions obtained a hundred years ago was not so much to "make people think" as to remind them of what they already thought (and again we are speaking comparatively). The oratorical rostrum, like the church, was less of a place for fresh instruction than for steady inculcation. And the orator, like the minister, was one who spoke from an eminent degree of conviction. Paradoxically, the speaker of this vanished period had more freedom to maneuver than has his emancipated successor. Man is free in proportion as his surroundings have a determinate nature, and he can plan his course with perfect reliance upon that determinateness. It is an admitted axiom that we have rules in one place so that we can have liberty in another; we put certain things in charge of habit so as to be free in areas where we prize freedom. Manifestly one is not "free" when one has to battle for one's position at every moment of time. This interrelationship of freedom and organization is one of the permanent conditions of existence, so that it has been said even that perfect freedom is perfect compliance ("one commands nature by obeying her").

In the province we are considering, man is free to the extent that he knows that nature is, what God expects, what he himself is capable of. Freedom moves on a set of presuppositions just as a machine moves on a set of ball bearings which themselves preserve definite locus. It is when these presuppositions are tampered with that men begin to grow concerned about their freedom. One can well imagine that the tremendous self-consciousness about freedom today, which we note in almost every utterance of public men, is evidence that this crucial general belief is threatened. It is no mere paradox to say that when they cry liberty, they mean belief—the belief that sets one free from prior concerns. A corroborating evidence is that fact that nearly all large pleas for liberty heard today conclude with more or less direct appeals for unity.

We may now return to our more direct concern with rhetoric. Since according to this demonstration oratory speaks from an eminence and has a freedom of purview, its syllogism is the "rhetorical syllogism" mentioned by Demetrius—the enthymeme.[4] It may not hurt to state that this is the syllogism with one of the three propositions missing. Such a syllogism

---

4. *On Style* (Cambridge: Harvard University Press, 1946), p. 321.

can be used only when the audience is willing to supply the missing proposition. The missing proposition will be "in their hearts," as it were; it will be their agreement upon some fundamental aspect of the issue being discussed. If it is there, the orator does not have to supply it; if it is not there, he may not be able to get it in any way—at least not as orator. Therefore the use of the rhetorical syllogism is good concrete evidence that the old orator relied upon the existence of uncontested terms or fixations of belief in the minds of his hearers. The orator was logical, but he could dispense with being a pure logician because that third proposition had been established for him.

These two related considerations, the accepted term and the conception of oratory as a body of judicious conclusions upon common evidence, go far toward explaining the quality of spaciousness. Indeed, to say that oratory has "spaciousness" is to risk redundancy once the nature of oratory is understood. Oratory is "spacious" in the same way that liberal education is liberal; and a correlation can be shown between the decline of liberal education (the education of a freeman) and the decline of oratory. It was one of Cicero's observations that the orator performs at "the focal point at which all human activity is ultimately reviewed"; and Cicero is, for connected reasons, a chief source of our theory of liberal education.[5]

Thus far we have rested our explanation on the utility of the generalized style, but this is probably much too narrow an account. There is also an aesthetic of the generalization,

---

5. See Norman J. DeWitt, "The Humanist Should Look to the Law," *Journal of General Education*, IV (January, 1950), 149. Although it is not our concern here, it probably could be shown that the essential requirements of oratory themselves depend upon a certain organization of society, such as an aristocratic republicanism. When Burke declares that a true natural aristocracy "is formed out of a class of legitimate presumptions, which, taken as generalities, must be admitted for actual truths" (*Works* [London, 1853–64], III, 85–86) my impression is that he has in mind something resembling our "uncontested term." The "legitimate presumptions" are the settled things which afford the plane of maneuver.

which we must now proceed to explore. Let us pause here momentarily to re-define our impression upon hearing the old orator. The feature which we have been describing as spaciousness may be translated, with perhaps a slight shift of viewpoint, as opacity. The passages we have inspected, to recur to our examples, are opaque in that we cannot see through them with any sharpness. And it was no doubt the intention of the orator that we should not see through them in this way. The "moral magnifying glass" of Craddock's General Vayne made objects larger, but it did not make them clearer. It rather had the effect of blurring lines and obscuring details.

We are now in position to suggest that another factor in the choice of the generalized phrase was aesthetic distance. There is an aesthetic, as well as a moral, limit to how close one may approach an object; and the forensic artists of the epoch we describe seem to have been guided by this principle of artistic decorum. Aesthetic distance is, of course, an essential of aesthetic treatment. If one sees an object from too close, one sees only its irregularities and protuberances. To see an object rightly or to see it as a whole, one has to have a proportioned distance from it. Then the parts fall into a meaningful pattern, the dominant effect emerges, and one sees it "as it really is." A prurient interest in closeness and a great remoteness will both spoil the view. To recall a famous example in literature, neither Lilliputian nor Brobdingnagian is man as we think we know him.

Thus it can be a sign not only of philosophical ignorance but also of artistic bad taste to treat an object familiarly or from a near proximity. At the risk of appearing fanciful we shall say that objects have not only their natures but their rights, which the orator is bound to respect, since he is in large measure the ethical teacher of society. By maintaining this distance with regard to objects, art manages to "idealize" them in a very special sense. One does not mean by this that it necessarily elevates them or transfigures them, but it certainly does keep out a kind of officious detail which would only lower the general effect. What the artistic procedure tends to do, then, is to give us a "generic" picture, and much the same can be said about oratory. The true orator has little concern with singularity—or, to recall again a famous instance, with the wart on Cromwell's face—because the singular is the impertinent. Only the generic belongs, and by obvious connection the language of the generic is a general language. In the old style, presentation kept distances which had, as one of their purposes, the obscuring of details. It would then have appeared the extreme of bad taste to particularize in the manner which has since, especially in certain areas of journalism, become a literary vogue. It would have been beyond the pale to refer, in anything intended for the public view, to a certain cabinet minister's false teeth or a certain congressman's shiny dome. Aesthetically, this was not the angle of vision from which one takes in the man, and there is even the question of epistemological truthfulness. Portrait painters know that still, and journalists knew it a hundred years ago.

It will be best to illustrate the effect of aesthetic distance. I have chosen a passage from the address delivered by John C. Breckinridge, Vice-President of the United States, on the occasion of the removal of the Senate from the Old to the New Chamber, January 4, 1859. The moment was regarded as solemn, and the speaker expressed himself as follows:

And now the strifes and uncertainties of the past are finished. We see around us on every side the proofs of stability and improvement. This Capitol is worthy of the Republic. Noble public buildings meet the view on every hand. Treasures of science and the arts begin to accumulate. As this flourishing city enlarges, it testifies to the wisdom and forecast that dictated the plan of it. Future generations will not be disturbed with questions concerning the center of population or of territory, since the steamboat, the railroad and the telegraph have made communication almost instantaneous. The spot is sacred by a thousand memories, which are so many pledges that the city of Washington, founded by him and bearing his revered name, with its beautiful site, bounded by picturesque eminences, and the broad Potomac, and lying within view of his home and his tomb, shall remain forever the political capital of the United States.

At the close of the address, he said:

And now, Senators, we leave this memorable chamber, bearing with us, unimpaired, the Constitution received from our forefathers. Let us cherish it with grateful acknowledgments of the Divine Power who controls the destinies of empires and whose goodness we adore. The structures reared by man yield to the corroding tooth of time. These marble walls must molder into ruin; but the principles of constitutional liberty, guarded by wisdom and virtue, unlike material elements, do not decay. Let us devoutly trust that another Senate in another age shall bear to a new and larger Chamber, the Constitution vigorous and inviolate, and that the last generations of posterity shall witness the deliberations of the Representatives of American States still united, prosperous, and free.[6]

We shall hardly help noting the prominence of "opaque" phrases. "Proofs of stability and improvement"; "noble public buildings"; "treasures of science and the arts"; "this flourishing city"; "a thousand memories"; "this beautiful site"; and "structures reared by man" seem outstanding examples. These all express objects which can be seen only at a distance of time or space. In three instances, it is true, the speaker mentions things of which his hearers might have been immediately and physically conscious, but they receive an appropriately generalized reference. The passage admits not a single intrusive detail, nor is anything there supposed to have a superior valid-

---

6. *Address Preceding the Removal of the Senate from the Old to the New Chamber: Delivered in the Senate of the United States, January 4, 1859* (Washington, 1859), (Printed at the Office of the Congressional Globe), pp. 5, 7.

ity or probativeness because it is present visibly or tangibly. The speech is addressed to the mind, and correspondingly to the memory.[7] The fact that the inclusiveness was temporal as well as spatial has perhaps special significance for us. This "continuity of the past with the present" gave a dimension which our world seems largely to have lost; and this dimension made possible a different pattern of selection. It is not experiential data which creates a sense of the oneness of experience. It is rather an act of mind; and the practice of periodically bringing the past into a meditative relationship with the present betokens an attitude toward history. In the chapter on Lincoln we have shown that an even greater degree of remoteness is discernible in the First and Second Inaugural Addresses, delivered at a time when war was an ugly present reality. And furthermore, at Gettysburg, Lincoln spoke in terms so "generic" that it is almost impossible to show that the speech is not a eulogy of the men in gray as well as the men in blue, inasmuch as both made up "those who struggled here." Lincoln's faculty of transcending an occasion is in fact only this ability to view it from the right distance, or to be wisely generic about it.

We are talking here about things capable of extremes, and there is a degree of abstraction which results in imperception; but barring those cases which everyone recognizes as beyond bounds, we should reconsider the idea that such generalization is a sign of impotence. The distinction does not lie between those who are near life and those who are remote from it, but between pertinence and impertinence. The intrusive detail so prized by modern realists does not belong in a picture which is a picture of something. One of the senses of "seeing" is metaphorical, and if one gets too close to the object, one can no longer in this sense "see." It is the *theoria* of the mind

---

7. There is commentary in the fact that the long commemorative address, with its assembled memories, was a distinctive institution of nineteenth-century America. Generalizations and "distance" were on such occasions the main resources.

as well as the work of the senses which creates the final picture. One can show this through an instructive contrast with modern journalism, particularly that of the *Time* magazine variety. A considerable part of its material, and nearly all of its captions, are made up of what we have defined as "impertinences." What our forensic artist of a century ago would have regarded as lacking significance is in these media presented as the pertinent because it is very near the physical manifestation of the event. And the reversal has been complete, because what for this artist would have been pertinent is there treated as impertinent since it involves matter which the average man does not care to reflect upon, especially under the conditions of newspaper reading. Thus even the epistemology which made the old oratory possible is being relegated.

We must take notice in this connection that the lavish use of detail is sometimes defended on the ground that it is illustration. The argument runs that illustration is a visual aid to education, and therefore an increased use of illustration contributes to that informing of the public which journals acknowledge as their duty. But a little reflection about the nature of illustration will show where this idea is treacherous. Illustration, as already indicated, implies that something is being illustrated, so that in the true illustration we will have a conjunction of mind and pictorial manifestation. But now, with brilliant technological means, the tendency is for manifestation to outrun the idea, so that the illustrations are vivid rather than meaningful or communicative. Thus, whereas today the illustration is looking for an idea to express, formerly the idea was the original; and it was looking, often rather fastidiously, for some palpable means of representation. The idea condescended, one might say, from an empyrean, to suffer illustrative embodiment.

To make this difference more real, let us study an example of the older method of illustration. The passage below examined is from an address by Rufus Choate on "The Position and Function of the American Bar as an Element of Conservatism

in the State," delivered before the Law School in Cambridge,
July 3, 1845.

But with us the age of this mode and degree of reform is over; its
work is done. The passage of the sea; the occupation and culture
of a new world, the conquest of independence—these were our
eras, these our agency of reform. In our jurisprudence of liberty,
which guards our person from violence and our goods from plun-
der, and which forbids the whole power of the state itself to take
the ewe lamb, or to trample on a blade of grass of the humblest
citizen without adequate remuneration: which makes every dwell-
ing large enough to shelter a human life its owner's castle which
winds and rain may enter, but which the government cannot,—in
our written constitution, whereby the people, exercising an act of
sublime self-restraint, have intended to put it out of their power
forever to be passionate, tumultuous, unwise, unjust, whereby they
have intended, by means of a system of representation, by means
of the distribution of government into departments independent,
coordinate for checks and balances; by a double chamber of legislation, by the establishment of a fundamental and permanent
organic law; by the organization of a judiciary whose function,
whose loftiest function it is to test the legislation of the day by the
standard of all time,—constitutions, whereby all these means they
have intended to secure a government of laws, not of men, of reason, not of will; of justice, not of fraud,—in that grand dogma of
equality,—equality of right, of burthens, of duty, of privileges, and
of chances, which is the very mystery of our social being—to the
Jews a stumbling block; to the Greeks foolishness,—our strength,
our glory,—in that liberty which we value not solely because it is
a natural right of man; not solely because it is a principle of individual energy and a guaranty of national renown; not at all because
it attracts a procession and lights a bonfire, but because, when
blended with order, attended by law, tempered by virtue, graced by
culture, it is a great practical good; because in her right hand are
riches and honor and peace, because she has come down from her
golden and purple cloud to walk in brightness by the weary ploughman's side, and whisper in his ear as he casts his seed with tears,
that the harvest which frost and mildew and cankerworm shall
spare, the government shall spare also; in our distribution into

separate and kindred states, not wholly independent, not quite identical, in "the wide arch of ranged empire" above—these are they in which the fruits of our age and our agency of reform are embodied; and these are they by which, if we are wise,—if we understand the things that belong to our peace—they may be perpetuated.[8]

We note in passing the now familiar panorama. One must view matters from a height to speak without pause of such things as "occupation and culture of a new world," "conquest of independence," and "fundamental and permanent organic law." Then we note that when the orator feels that he must illustrate, the illustration is not through the impertinent concrete case, but through the poeticized figment. At the close of the passage, where the personification of liberty is encountered, we see in clearest form the conventionalized image which is the traditional illustration. Liberty, sitting up in her golden and purple cloud, descends "to walk in brightness by the weary ploughman's side." In this flatulent utterance there is something so typical of method (as well as indicative of the philosophy of the method) that one can scarcely avoid recalling that this is how the gods of classical mythology came down to hold discourse with mortals; it is how the god of the Christian religion came into the world for the redemption of mankind; it is how the *logos* is made incarnate. In other words, this kind of manifestation from above is, in our Western tradition, an archetypal process, which the orators of that tradition are likely to follow implicitly. The idea is supernal; it may be brought down for representation; but casual, fortuitous, individual representations are an affront to it. Consequently the representations are conventionalized images, and work with general efficacy.

This thought carries us back to our original point, which is

<hr>

8. *The Position and Function of the American Bar, as an Element of Conservatism in the State: An Address Delivered before the Law School in Cambridge,* July 3, 1845. From *Addresses and Orations of Rufus Choate* (Boston: Little, Brown, 1891), pp. 141–43.

that standards of pertinence and impertinence have very deep foundations, and that one may reveal one's whole system of philosophy by the stand one takes on what is pertinent. We have observed that a powerful trend today is toward the unique detail and the illustration of photographic realism, and this tendency claims to be more knowledgeable about reality. In the older tradition which we set out to examine, the abstracted truth and the illustration which is essentially a construct held a like favor. It was not said, because there was no contrary style to make the saying necessary, but it was certainly felt that these came as near the truth as one gets, if one admits the existence of non-factual kinds of truth. The two sides do not speak to one another very well across the gulf, but it is certainly possible to find, and it would seem to be incumbent upon scholars to find, a conception broad enough to define the difference.

One further clue we have as to how the orator thought and how he saw himself. There will be observed in most speeches of this era a stylization of utterance. It is this stylization which largely produces their declamatory quality. At the same time, as we begin to infer causes, we discover the source of its propriety; the orator felt that he was speaking for corporate humanity. He had a sense of stewardship which would today appear one of the presumptions earlier referred to. The individual orator was not, except perhaps in certain postures, offering an individual testimonial. He was the mouthpiece for a collective brand of wisdom which was not to be delivered in individual accents. We may suppose that the people did not resent the stylizations of the orator any more than now they resent the stylizations of the Bible. "That is the way God talks." The deity should be above mere novelties of expression, transparent devices of rhetoric, or importunate appeals for attention. It is enough for him to be earnest and truthful; we will rise to whatever patterns of expression it has pleased him to use. Stylization indicates an attitude which will not concede too much, or certainly will not concede weakly or complacently. As in point of historical sequence the language of political discourse succeeded that of the sermon, some of the latter's dignity and self-confidence persisted in the way of formalization. Thus when the orator made gestures toward the occasion, they were likely to be ceremonious rather than personal or spontaneous, the oration itself being an occasion of "style." The modern listener is very quick to detect a pattern of locution, but he is prone to ascribe it to situations of weakness rather than of strength.

Of course oratory of the broadly ruminative kind is acceptable only when we accredit someone with the ability to review our conduct, our destiny, and the causes of things in general. If we reach a condition in which no man is believed to have this power, we will accordingly be impatient with that kind of discourse. It should not be overlooked that although the masses in any society are comparatively ill-trained and ignorant, they are very quick to sense attitudes, through their native capacity as human beings. When attitudes change at the top of society, they are able to see that change long before they are able to describe it in any language of their own, and in fact they can see it without ever doing that. The masses thus follow intellectual styles, and more quickly than is often supposed, so that, in this particular case, when a general skepticism of predication sets in among the leaders of thought, the lower ranks are soon infected with the same thing (though one must make allowance here for certain barriers to cultural transmission constituted by geography and language). This principle will explain why there is no more appetite for the broadly reflective discourse among the general public of today than among the élite. The stewardship of man has been hurt rather than helped by the attacks upon natural right, and at present nobody knows who the custodians (in the old sense of "watchers") are. Consequently it is not easy for a man to assume the ground requisite for such a discourse. Speeches today either are made for entertainment, or they are political speeches for political ends. And the chief characteristic of the speech for political ends is that it is made for immediate effect, with the smallest regard for what is politically true. Whereas formerly its burden was what the people believed or had experienced, the burden now tends to be what they wish to hear. The increased reliance upon slogans and catchwords, and the increased use of the argument from contraries (*e.g.*, "the thing my opponent is doing will be welcomed by the Russians") are prominent evidences of the trend.[9]

Lastly, the old style may be called, in comparison with what has succeeded, a polite style. Its very diffuseness conceals a respect for the powers and limitations of the audience. Bishop Whatley has observed that highly concentrated expression may be ill suited to persuasion because the majority of the people are not capable of assimilating concentrated thought. The principle can be shown through an analogy with nutrition. It is known that diet must contain a certain amount of roughage. This roughage is not food in the sense of nutriment; its function is to dilute or distend the real food in such a way that it can be most readily assimilated. A concentrate of food is, therefore, not enough, for there has to be a certain amount of inert matter to furnish bulk. Something of a very similar nature operates in discourse. When a piece of oratory intended for a public occasion impresses us as distended, which is to say, filled up with repetition, periphrasis, long grammatical forms, and other impediments to directness, we should recall that the diffuseness all this produces may have a purpose. The orator may have made a close calculation of the receptive powers of his audience and have ordered his style to meet that, while continuing to "sound good" at every point. This represents a form of consideration for the audience. There exists quite commonly today, at the opposite pole, a syncopated style. This style, with its suppression of beats and its consequent effect of hurrying over things, does not show that type

---

9. A distinction must be made between "uncontested terms" and slogans. The former are parts of the general mosaic of belief; the latter are uncritical aspirations, or at the worst, shibboleths.

of consideration. It does not give the listener the roughage of verbiage to chew on while meditating the progress of the thought. Here again "spaciousness" has a quite rational function in enforcing a measure, so that the mind and the sentiments too can keep up with the orator in his course.

Perhaps this is as far as we can go in explaining the one age to another. We are now in position to realize that the archaic formalism of the old orator was a structure imparted to his speech by a logic, an aesthetic, and an epistemology. As a logician he believed in the deduced term, or the term whose empirical support is not at the moment visible. As an aesthetician he believed in distance, and that not merely to soften outline but also to evoke the true picture, which could be obscured by an injudicious and prying nearness. As an epistemologist he believed, in addition to the foregoing, that true knowledge somehow had its source in the mind of minds, for which we are on occasion permitted to speak a part. All this gave him a peculiar sense of stature. He always talked like a big man. Our resentment comes from a feeling that with all his air of confidence he could not have known half as much as we know. But everything depends on what we mean by knowing; and the age or the man who has the true conception of that will have, as the terms of the case make apparent, the key to every other question.

Chapter VIII

THE RHETORIC
OF SOCIAL SCIENCE

ONE OF THE serious problems of our age is the question of how scientific information, which is largely the product of special tools of investigation, shall be communicated to the non-specialist world. A few sciences operate in fields of theory so abstract that they can create their own symbology, and most of what they transmit to the public will be in the form of highly generalized translation. But there are other sciences whose very success depends upon some public understanding of what they are trying to solve, and these are faced with peculiar problems of communication. None are in so difficult a position as social science. The social sciences have been, since their institution, jealous of their status as science, and that is perhaps understandable. But their data is the everyday life of man in society, and naturally if there is an area of scientific discovery upon which the general public should be posted, it is just this one of the laws of social phenomena. Caught between this desire to remain scientific and the necessity of public expression, most social scientists are in a dilemma. They have not devised (and possibly they cannot devise) their own symbology to rival that of the mathematician and physicist. On the other hand, they have not set themselves to learn the principles of sound rhetorical exposition. The result is that the publications of social scientists contain a large amount of conspicuously poor writing, which is now under growing attack.[1] Some of these attacks have been perceptive

1. *E. g.*, Samuel T. Williamson, "How to Write Like a Social Scientist," *Saturday Review of Literature*, XXX, No. 40 (October 4, 1947), 17.

as well as witty; but I feel that no one has yet made the point which most needs making, which is that the social scientists will never write much better until they make terms with some of the traditional rules of rhetoric.

I propose in the study which follows to ignore the isolated small faults and instead to analyze the sources of pervasive vices. I shall put the inquiry in the form of a series of questions, which lead to cardinal principles of conception and of choice.

I

Does the writing of social scientists suffer from a primary equivocation? The charge against social science writing which would be most widely granted is that it fails to convince us that it deals clearly with realities. This impression may lead to the question of whether the social scientist knows what he is talking about. Now this is a serious, not a frivolous, question, involving matters of logic and epistemology; it is a question, furthermore, that one finds the social scientists constantly putting to themselves and answering in a variety of ways. Any field of study is liable to a similar interrogation; in this instance it merely asks whether those who interpret social behavior in scientific terms are aware of the kind of data they are handling. Are they dealing with facts, or concepts, or evaluations, or all three? The answer given to this question will have a definite bearing upon their problem of expression, and let us see how this can happen in a concrete instance.

We have had much to say in preceding chapters about the distinction between positive and dialectical terms; and nowhere has the ignoring of this distinction had worse results than in the literature of social science. We have seen, to review briefly, that the positive term designates something existing simply in the objective world: the chair, the tree, the farm. Arguments over positive terms are not arguments in the true sense, since the point at issue is capable of immediate and public settlement, just as one might settle an "argument" over the width of a room by bringing in a publicly-agreed-upon yard-stick. Consequently a rhetoric of positive terms is a rhetoric of simple description, which requires only powers of accurate observation and reporting.

It is otherwise with dialectical terms. These are terms stand-ing for concepts, which are defined by their negatives or their privations. "Justice" is a dialectical term which is defined by "injustice"; "social improvement" is made meaningful by the use of "privation of social improvement." To say that a family has an income of $800.00 a year is positive; to say that the same family is underprivileged is dialectical. It can be under-privileged only with reference to families which have more privileges. So it goes with the whole range of terms which reflect judgments of value; "unjust," "poor," "underpaid," "un-desirable" are all terms which depend on something more than the external world for their significance.

Now here is where the social scientist crosses a divide that he seldom acknowledges and often seems unaware of. One cannot use the dialectical term in the same manner as one uses the positive term because the dialectical term always leaves one committed to something. It is a truth easily seen that all dialectical terms make presumptions from the plain fact that they are "positional" terms. A writer no sooner employs one than he is engaged in an argument. To say that the universe is purposeless is to join in argument with all who say it is pur-poseful. To say that a certain social condition is inequitable is to ally oneself with the reformers and against the standpat-ters. In all such cases the presumption has to do with the scope of the term and with its relationship to its opposite, and these can be worked out only through the dialectical method we have analyzed in other chapters. When the reader of social science comes to such terms, he is baffled because he has not been warned of the presumptions on which they rest. Or, to be more exact, he has not been prepared for presumptions at all. He finds himself reading at a level where the facts have been subsumed, and where the exposition is a process of ad-

justing categories. The writer has passed with indifference
from what is objectively true to what is morally or imagina-
tively true. The reader's uneasiness comes from a feeling that
the categories themselves are the things which should have
been examined. Just here, however, may lie the crux of the
difficulty.

It begins to look as though the social scientist working with
his regular habits is actually a dialectician without a dialectical basis. His dilemma is that he can neither use his terms
with the simple directness of the natural scientist pointing to
physical factors, nor with the assurance of a philosopher who
has some source for their meaning in the system from which he
begins his deduction. Or, the social scientist is trying to characterize the world positively in terms which can be made good
only dialectically. He can never make them good dialectically
as long as he is by theory entirely committed to empiricism.
This explains why to the ordinary beholder there seem to
be so many smuggled assumptions in the literature of social
science. It will explain, moreover, why so much of its expression is characterized by diffuseness and by that verbosity
which is certain to afflict a dialectic without a metaphysic or
an ontology. This uncertainty of the social scientist about the
nature of his datum often leads him to treat empirical situations as if they carried moral sanction, and then to turn around
and treat some point of contemporary mores—which is by
definition a "moral" question—as if it had only empirical aspects. In direct consequence, when the social scientist should
be writing "positively," like a crack newspaper reporter, one
finds him writing like Hegel, and, when the stage of his exposition might warrant his writing more or less like Hegel, one
finds him employing dialectical terms as if they had positive
designations.

Paradoxically, his very reverence for facts may tend to make
him sound like Hegel or some other master of categorical
thinking. Anyone sampling the literature of social science cannot fail to be impressed with the proportion of space given to

definition. Indeed, one of the most convincing claims of the
science is that our present-day knowledge of man is defective
because our definitions are simplistic. His behavior is much
more varied than the unscientific suppose; and therefore a
central objective of social study is definition, which will take
this variety into account and supplant our present "prejudiced" definitions. With this in mind, the social scientist toils
in library or office to prepare the best definitions he can of
human nature, of society, and of psychosocial environment.

The danger for him in this laudable endeavor seems two-
fold. First, one must remark that the language of definition is
inevitably the language of generality because only the gen-
eralizable is definable. Singulars and individuals can be described but not defined; e.g., one can define man, but one can
only describe Abraham Lincoln. The greater, then, his solici-
tude for the factual and the concrete, the more irresistibly is
he borne in the direction of abstract language, which alone
will encompass his collected facts. His dissertations on human
society begin with obeisance to facts, but the logic of his being
a scientist condemns him to abstraction. He is forced toward
the position of the proverbial revolutionary, who loves mankind but has little charity for those particular specimens of
it with whom he must associate.

In the second place and more importantly, the definition of
non-empirical terms is itself a dialectical process. All such
definition takes the form of an argument which must prove
that the *definiendum* is one thing and not another thing. The
limits of the definition are thus the boundary between the
things and the not-thing. Someone might inquire at this stage
of our account whether the natural scientists, who must also
define, are not equally liable under this point of the argument.
The distinction is that definitions in natural science have a different ontological basis. The properties about which they generalize exist not in logical connection but in empirical conjunction, as when "mammal," "vertebrate," and "quadruped"
are used to distinguish the genus *Felis*. The doctrine of "nat-

ural kinds" thus remains an empirical classification, as does the traditional classification of elements.[2] Consequently the genus *Felis* has a reality in the form of compresent positive attributes which "slum" cannot have. The establishment of the genus is not a matter of negating or depriving other classes, but of naming what is there. On the other hand one could never arrive positivistically at a definition of "slum" because its meaning is contingent upon judgment (and theoretically our standard of living might move up to where Westchester, Grosse Point, and Winnetka are regarded as slums). Thus "slum" no more exists objectively than does "bad weather." There are collections of sticks and stones which the dialectician may call "slums," just as there are processions of the elements which he may call "bad." But these are positive things only in a reductionist equation. Of course, the natural scientist works always with reductionist equations; but the social scientist, unless he is an extreme materialist, must work with the full equation.

It is a grave imputation, but at the heart of the social scientist's unsatisfactory expression lies this equivocation. Remedy here can come only with a clearer defining of province and of responsibility.

II

Is social science writing marred by "pedantic empiricism"? The natural desire of everyone to carry away something from his reading encounters in this literature curious obstacles. Its authors often seem unduly coy about their conclusions. After the reader has been escorted on an extensive tour of facts and definitions, he is likely to be told that little can be affirmed at this stage of the inquiry. So it is that, however much we read, we are made to feel that what we are reading is preliminary.

2. See Bertrand Russell, "The Postulate of Natural Kinds or of Limited Variety," *Human Knowledge: Its Scope and Limits* (New York: Simon & Schuster, 1948), pp. 438–44.

We come almost to look for a formula at the close of a social science monograph which takes an excessively modest view of its achievement while expressing the hope that someone else may come along and do something with the data there offered. Burgess and Cottrell's *Predicting Success or Failure in Marriage* provides an illustration. After presenting their case, the authors say: "In this study, as in many others, the most significant contribution is not to be found in any one finding but in the degree to which the study opens up a new field to further research."[3] Again, from an article appearing in *Social Forces:* "The findings here mentioned are merely suggestive; and they are offered in no sense as proof of our hypothesis of folk-urban personality differences. The implementation of the analysis given here would demand a field project incorporating the type of methodological consciousness advocated above. Thus we need to utilize standard projective devices, but must be prepared to develop, in terms of situational demands, additional analytic instruments."[4] And Herman C. Beyle in a chapter on the data and method of political science, which constitute the underpinning of his whole study, can only say that "the foregoing comments on the data and technology of political science have been offered as most tentative statements intended to provide a background for the testing and application of the technique here proposed, that of attribute-cluster-bloc identification and analysis."[5] "Most tentative" becomes a sort of leitmotiv. Everything sounds like a prolegomenon to the real thing. Exclamations that social scientists are taking in one another's washing or are only trying to make work for themselves are inspired by this kind of performance.

But, even after one has made allowance for the fact that

---

3. (New York: Prentice-Hall, 1939), p. 349.

4. Melvin Seeman, "An Evaluation of Current Approaches to Personality Differences in Folk and Urban Societies," *Social Forces*, XXV (December, 1946), 165.

5. *Identification and Analysis of Attribute-Cluster-Blocs* (Chicago: University of Chicago Press, 1931), p. 214.

social science is not one of the exact sciences and that its dis-
ciples work in a field where induction is far from complete,
their fear of commitment still seems obsessive. They could at
least have the courage of the facts which they have accumulated. Virtually everyone who is seeking scientific enlightenment on this level knows that conclusions are given in the light
of evidence available, and that hypothesis always extends
some distance beyond what is directly observable. Indeed,
everyone makes use of the method of scientific investigation, as
T. H. Huxley liked to assure his audiences, but not everyone
finds necessary such an armor of qualifications as is likely to
appear here: "On the basis of available evidence, it is not unreasonable to suppose"; "It may not be improbable in view of
these findings"; "The present survey would seem to indicate."
All these rhetorical contortions are forms of needless hedging.

It would be a different matter if such formulas of reserva-
tion made the conclusion more precise. But in the majority of
cases it could be shown that the conclusion is obvious enough
in terms of the discussion itself, and they serve only to make
it sound timid. These scholars move to a tune of "induction
never ends," and their scholarship often turns into a pedantic
empiricism. They seem to be waiting for the fact that will
bring with it the revelation. But that fact will never arrive;
experience does not tell us what we are experiencing, and at
some point they are going to have to give names to their findings—even at the expense of becoming dialecticians.

If the needlessly hedged statement is one result of pedantic
empiricism, another occurs in what might be called "pedantic
analysis." This is analysis for analysis' sake, with no real
thought of relevance or application or, indeed, of a resynthesis
which might redeem the whole undertaking. Just as it is assumed that an endless collection of data will necessarily yield
fruits, so it is assumed that a remorseless partitioning will illu-
minate. But analysis can be carried so far that it seems to lose
all bearing upon points at issue. The writer shows himself a
sort of *virtuoso* at analysis, and one feels that his real interest

lies in demonstrating how thoroughly a method can be followed. Let us look, for example, at a passage from an article
entitled "Courtship as a Social Institution in the United States,
1930–1945." The author has said that activities of courtship
show different patterns and that sometimes the patterns need
to be harmonized:

To be compatible, patterns should be adapted to the following
components: (1) the *hominid component,* which is the biological
human being; (2) the *social component,* which includes the potentialities for social relations as they are affected by "the number of
human beings in the situation, their distribution in space, their
ages, their sex, their native ability to interstimulate and interact,
the interference of environmental hindrances or helps, and the
presence and amount of certain types of social equipment"; (3)
the *environmental component,* or all the "natural" features of the
situation except the hominid, the social, the psychological and
artifactual components; it includes topography, physiography,
flora, fauna, weather, geology, soil, etc.; (4) the *psychological
component,* defined as the principles involving the acquisition and
performance of human customs not adequately explained on purely
biological principles; (5) the *artifactual component,* which consists collectively of the material results and adjuncts of human
customary activities.[6]

It is not always safe for the layman to generalize about the
value of specific sociological findings, but I am inclined to
think that this is verbiage, resulting from analysis pushed beyond any useful purpose. There is a real if obscure relationship
between the vitality of what one is saying and the palatability
of one's rhetoric. No rhythm, no *tournure* of phiase, no archi-
tecture of the sentences could make this a good piece of writing, for its content lies on the outer fringe of significance. It
is the nature of such pedantry to habit itself in a harsh and
crabbed style.

6. Donald L. Taylor, "Courtship as a Social Institution in the United
States, 1930–1945," *Social Forces,* XXV (October, 1946), 68.

The primary step in literary composition is *invention*, or the discovering of something to talk about. No writer is finally able to make good the claim that his subject matter is one thing and his style of expression another; the subject matter enters into the expression inevitably and extensively, although sometimes in ways too subtle for elucidation. What of the invention of this passage? If we take the word in its etymological sense of "finding," are not these distinctions "findings" for findings' sake? Analysis carried to such a humorless extreme reflects discredit upon the very principle of division which was employed.

It may appear contradictory to call the social scientist a "tendentious dialectician" and a "pedantic empiricist" at the same time. But the contradiction is inherent in his situation and merely expresses the equivocation found earlier. In all likelihood the empiricism is an attempt to compensate for the dialectic. If a writer feels guilty about his dialectic exercises (his definitions), he may seek to counterweight them with long empirical inquiries. The object of the empirical analysis is primarily to give the work a scientific aspect and only secondarily to prove something. In fact, this is almost the pattern of inferior social science literature.

III

Does social science writing suffer from a melioristic bias? This question directs our attention to the matter of vocabulary. There is danger in criticising any writer's vocabulary through application of simple principles, because demands vary widely. For some purposes a small vocabulary of denotative terms will be satisfactory. Other purposes cannot be adequately met without a large and learned vocabulary which may, incidentally, sound pretentious. Our question then becomes whether the ends of social science are being well served by the means employed. For example, social scientists are often charged with addiction to polysyllabic vocabulary. Other men of learning show the same addiction, but there are special reasons for weighing critically the polysyllabic diction of social scientists.

Of course, when one faces the issue concretely, one discovers that there is no single standard by which a word is classified "big." Some words are called "big" because they actually have four or five syllables and hence are measurably so; other words of one or two syllables are called "big" because, coming out of technical or scientific vocabularies, they are unfamiliar to the average man;[7] others, actually no longer, are called "big" because of the company they keep; that is to say, they are words of learned or dignified association. Sometimes a word seems big when it is simply too pretentious for the kind of thing it is describing. Readers of H. L. Mencken will recall that he obtained many of his best satirical effects by describing what was essentially picayune or tawdry in a vocabulary of grandiloquence.

A cursory inspection will show that social scientists are given to words which are "big" in yet another respect: they have a Latin origin. Even in analysis of simple phenomenon the reader comes to expect a parade of terms which seem to go by on stilts, as if it were important to keep from touching the ground. Without raising questions of semantic theory, one inclines to wonder about their relationship to their referents. In course of time one may come to suspect that the words employed are not dictated by the subject matter, but by some active principle out of sociological theory. To see whether that suspicion has a foundation, let us try a test on a specimen of this language.

The passage which will be used is fairly representative of the ordinary social science prose to be encountered in articles and reports. The subject is expressed in the title "Social Nearness among Welfare Institutions":

---

7. For example: "id," "ion," "alga."

It was noticed in the preceding sections that the social welfare organizational milieu presents an interdependence, a formal solidarity, a coerced feeling of unity. However divergent the specific objectives of each organization, theoretically they all have a common purpose, the care of the so-called underprivileged. Whether they execute what they profess or not is a different question and one which does not fall within the confines of these pages.[8]

There occur in this short excerpt about a dozen words of Latin origin for which equivalents of Anglo-Saxon (or old English, if the name is preferred) origin are available, and this without giving up presumably operational terms like "organizational" and "milieu."[9] In place of "noticed," why not "seen"? In place of "divergent," why not "unlike"? In place of "objective," why not "goal"? Instead of "execute what they profess," why not "do what they say"? Did these terms not suggest themselves to the writer, or were they deliberately passed by?

It might be arbitrary to insist that any one of these substitutes is better than the original, but the piling-up of such terms causes language to take on a special aspect. There are, of course, margins within which preference in terminology means little, but a preference for Latinate terms as marked as this must be, to employ one of their customary expressions, "significant."

That significance lies in the kind of attitude that social scientists must have in order to practice social science. It seems beyond dispute that all social science rests upon the assumption that man and society are improvable. That is its origin and its guiding impulse. The man who does not feel that social behavior and social institutions can be bettered through the application of scientific laws, or through some philosophy finding its basic support in them, is surely out of place in

---

8. Samuel H. Jameson, "Social Nearness among Welfare Institutions," *Sociology and Social Research*, XV (March–April, 1931), 322.

9. The natural scientists, too, use many Latinate terms, but these are chiefly "name" words, for which there are no real substitutes.

sociology. There would really be nothing for him to do. He could only sit on the sidelines and speculate dourly, like Nietzsche, or ironically, like Santayana. The very profession which the true social scientist adopts compels him to be a kind of a priori optimist. This is why a large part of social science writing displays a *melioristic bias*. It is under compulsion, often unconsciously felt, I am sure, to picture things a little better than they are. Such expression provides a kind of proof that its theories are "working."

An indubitable connection exists between the melioristic bias and a Latinate vocabulary. Even a moderate sensitivity to the overtones of language will tell one that diction of Latin derivation tends to be euphemistic. For this there seem to be both extrinsic and intrinsic causes. It is a commonplace of historical knowledge that after the Norman Conquest the Anglo-Saxons were forced into a servile role. They were sent into the fields to do chores for the Norman overlords, and Anglo-Saxon names have clung to the things with which they worked. Thus to the Anglo-Saxon in the field the animal was "cow"; to the Norman, when the same animal was served at his table, it was "beef" (L. *bos, bovis*). So "calf" is translated "veal"; "thegn" becomes "servant"; "folk" becomes "people," and so on. This distinction of common and elegant terms persists in an area of our vocabulary today. Another circumstance was that Latin for centuries constituted the language of learning and of the professions throughout Europe, and from the fourteenth century onward, there occurred a large amount of "learned borrowing."[10] This reflects the fact that those cultures which carried civility and *politesse* to highest perfection drew from a Latin source. Finally, I would suggest that the greater number of syllables in many Latinate terms is a factor in the effect. Whatever the complete explanation, the truth remains that to give a thing a Latinate name is to couple

---

10. See J. B. Greenough and G. L. Kittredge, *Words and Their Ways in English Speech* (New York, 1931), pp. 94–99.

it with social prestige and with the world of ideas, whereas to give it a name out of Anglo-Saxon is to forgo such dignifying associations. Thus "combat" sounds more dignified than "fight"; "labor" has resonances which "work" does not have; "impecunious" seems to indicate a more hopeful condition than "needy" or "penniless"; "involuntary separation" sounds less painful than "getting fired." The list could be extended indefinitely. With exceptions too few to make a difference, the Anglo-Saxon word is plain and workaday, whereas the word of Latin derivation seems to invest whatever it describes with a certain upward tendency. Of course, the Anglo-Saxon word has its potencies, but they are not those of the other. It seems to cling to the brute empirical fact, while its Latinate counterpart seems at once to become ideological, with perhaps a slight aura of hortation about it. Whenever one hears the average man condemning a piece of discourse as "flowery," it is most likely that he is pointing, with the only term at his command, to an excess of Latinate diction.

In the same connection, let us remember that the last few years have seen much newspaper wit at the expense of the language of government bureaucracy, which is even more responsive to the melioristic bias. The bureaucrat lives in a world where nothing is incorrigible; the solution to every contemporary difficulty waits only for the devising of some appropriate administrative machinery. Compared with him, the social scientist is a realist, for social science at least begins by admitting that many situations leave something to be desired. The bureaucrat's world is prim and proper and aseptic, and his language reflects it (perhaps one could say that the discourse of the bureaucrat is social science "politicalized"). At any rate, here we might profitably look at a specimen of bureaucratic parlance from Masterson and Phillips' *Federal Prose*, a recently published burlesque of official language. The authors posed for themselves as one exercise the problem of how a bureaucrat would express the ancient adage "Too many cooks spoil the broth." Their translation is a caricature, but, like caricature, it brings out the dominant features of the subject: "Undue multiplicity of personnel assigned either concurrently or consecutively to a single function involves deterioration of quality in the resultant product as compared with the product of the labor of an exact sufficiency of personnel."[11] One notices, first of all, the leap into polysyllabic diction, along with the total disappearance of those homely entities "cooks" and "broth." "Personnel," for example, is an abstract dignifier, and "resultant product" is safe, since it does not leave the writer on record as affirming that the concoction in question actually is broth. He is further protected by the expunging of "spoil," with its positive assertion, and he can hide behind the relativity of "deterioration of quality . . . as compared with. . . ."

Such language, when used to express the phenomenology of social and political behavior, gives a curious impression of being foreign to its subject matter. The impression of foreignness may be explained as follows. In all writing which has come to be regarded as wisdom about the human being, there is an undertone of the sardonic. Man at his best is a sort of caricature of himself, and even when we are eulogizing him for his finer attributes, there has to be a minor theme of depreciation, much as a vein of comedy weaves in and out of a great tragedy. The "great" actions of history appear either sublime or ridiculous, depending on one's standpoint, and it may be the part of sagacity to regard them as both at the same time. This note of the sardonic is found in biblical wisdom, in Plato's realism of situations, and even in Aristotle's dry categorizing. It appears in the *Federalist* papers,[12] as the authors, while debating political theory in high terms, kept a cagey eye upon economic man. Man is neither an angel nor any kind of disembodied spirit, and the attempt to treat him as such

11. James R. Masterson and Wendell Brooks Phillips, *Federal Prose: How to Write in and/or for Washington* (Chapel Hill: University of North Carolina Press, 1948), p. 10.

12. Cf., for example, Madison in No. 10.

only arouses our sense of the ridiculous. The comic animal must be there before we can grant that the representation is "true." The typical social science report, even when it discusses situations in which baseness and irrationality figure prominently, does not get in this ingredient. Every social fact may be serious, but not every social action is serious because action is not fully explainable without motive. It is this abstract man which causes some of us to wonder about the predications of an unhumanistic social science.

The remedy might be to employ, except where the necessity of conceptualizing makes it difficult, something nearer the language of the biblical parable (one shudders to think how our bureaucrat would render "A sower went forth to sow"), or the language of the best British journalism. I have often felt that writers on social science might learn a valuable lesson from the limpid prose of the *Manchester Guardian*. There one usually finds statement without eulogistic or dyslogistic tendency, adequacy without turgidity. It is perhaps the nearest thing we have in practice to that supposititious reality, objective language. There is some truth in the observation of John Peale Bishop that, whereas American English is more vigorous, English English is far more accurate. A good reportorial medium will be, to a considerable extent, an English English, and it will reflect something of the English genius for fact.

To sum up, the melioristic bias is a deflection toward language which glosses over reality without necessarily giving us a philosophic vocabulary. One could go so far as to say that such language is comparatively lacking in responsibility. It is the language that one expects from those who have become insulated or daintified. It carries a slight suggestion of denial of evil, which in lay circles, as in some ecclesiastical ones, is among the greatest heresies Perhaps the sociologist would inspire more confidence as a social physician if his language had more of the candor described above, and almost certainly he would get a better understanding of his diagnosis.

IV

Do the social scientists lose more than they gain by a distrust of metaphor? Dr. Johnson once remarked of Swift, "The rogue never hazards a metaphor," and that may well be the reaction of anyone who has plowed through the drab pages of a contemporary sociologist. It has long been suspected that sociologists and poets have little confidence in one another, and here their respective procedures come into complete contrast. The poet works mainly with metaphor, and the sociologist will have none of it. Which is right? Or, if each is doing instinctively the thing that is right for him, must we affirm that the works they produce are of very unequal importance?

One can readily see how the social scientist might be guided by the simple impression that, since metaphor characterizes the language of poetry, it has, for that very reason, no place in the language of science. Or, if he should become more analytical, he might conclude that metaphor, through its very operation of analogy or transference, implies the existence of a realm which positivistic study denies. To use metaphor, then, would be to pass over to the enemy. But he would be a very limited kind of sociologist, a sort of doctrinaire mechanist, not fully posted on all the resources open to scientific inquiry.

There are two more or less familiar theories of the nature of metaphor. One holds that metaphor is mere decoration. It is like the colored lights and gewgaws one hangs on a Christmas tree; the tree is an integral tree without them, but they do add sparkle and novelty and so are good things for such occasions. So the metaphors used in language are pleasurable accessories, which give it a certain charm and lift but which are supererogatory when one comes down to the business of understanding what is said. This theory has been fully discredited not only by those who have analyzed the language of poetry, but also by those who have gone furthest into the psychology of language itself and have explored the "meaning of meaning."

A second theory holds that metaphor is a useful concession to our feeble imagination. We are all children of Adam to the extent that we crave material embodiments. Even the most highly trained of us are wearied by long continuance of abstract communication; we want the thing brought down to earth so that we can see it. For the same reason that principles have to be put into fables for children, the abstract conceptions of modern science require figures for their popular expression. Thus the universe of Einstein is represented as "like" the surface of an orange; or the theory of entropy is illustrated by the figure of a desert on which Arabs are riding their camels hither and thither. From the standpoint of rhetoric, this theory has some validity. Visualization is an aid to seeing relationships, and there are rhetorical situations which demand some kind of picturization. Many skilled expositors will follow an abstract proposition with some easy figure which lets us down to earth or enables us to get a bearing. There is some value, then, in the "incarnation" of concepts. On this ground alone one could defend the use of metaphors in communication.[13]

There is yet another theory, now receiving serious attention, that metaphor is itself a means of discovery. Of course, metaphor is intended here in the broadest sense, requiring only some form of parallelism.[14] But when its essential nature is understood, it is hard to resist the thought that metaphor is one of the most important heuristic devices, leading us from a known to an unknown, but subsequently verifiable, fact of principle. Thus George de Santillana, writing on "Aspects of Scientific Rationalism in the Nineteenth Century," can de-

---

13. It is possible that there exists also a concrete understanding, which differs qualitatively from abstract or scientific understanding and is needed to supplement it, particularly when we are dealing with moral phenomena (see Andrew Bongiorno, "Poetry as an Educational Instrument," *Bulletin of the American Association of University Professors*, XXXIII [Autumn, 1947], 508–9).

14. Cf. Aristotle, *Rhetoric*, 1410 b: ". . . for when the poet calls old age 'stubble,' he produces in us a knowledge and information by means of a common genus; for both are past their prime."

clare, "There is never a 'strict induction' but contains a considerable amount of deduction, starting from points chosen analogically."[15] In other words, analogy formulates and to some extent directs the inquiry. Any investigation must start from certain minimal likenesses, and that may conceal the truth that some analogy lies at the heart of all assertion. Even Bertrand Russell is compelled to accept analogy as one of the postulates required to validate the scientific method because it provides the antecedent probability necessary to justify an induction.[16]

We might go so far as to admit the point of George Lundberg, who has given attention to the underlying theory of social science, that artists and philosophers make only "allegations" about the world, which scientists must put to the test.[17] For the inquiry may go from allegation to allegation, through a series of metaphorical constructs. This in no wise diminishes the role of metaphor but rather recognizes the role it has always had. If we should speak, for example of the "dance of life," we would be using a metaphor of considerable illuminating power, in that it rests upon a number of resemblances, some of which are hidden or profound. If we push it vigorously, we may be surprised at some of the insights which will turn up. Our naïve question, "What is it like?" which we ask of anything we are confronting for the first time, is the intellect's cry for help. Unless it is like something in some measure, we shall never get to understand it.

The usual student of literature is prone to feel that there is more social psychology in *Hamlet* than in a dozen volumes on the theory of the subject. Hamlet is a category, a kind of concrete universal; why would he yield less as a factor in an analysis than some operational definition? At least one social psychologist has felt no hesitation about employing this kind

15. *International Encyclopedia of Unified Science* (Chicago: University of Chicago Press, 1941), II, No. 8, 7.

16. *Op. cit.*, p. 487.

17. *Foundations of Sociology* (New York: Macmillan, 1939), p. 383.

of factor, the only difference being that his is Babbitt, of more recent creation. Ellsworth Faris, in developing a thesis that every person has several selves, presents his meaning as follows:

Moreover, whatever the list of personalities or roles may be, there is always room for one more, and indeed for many more. When war comes, Babbitt will probably be a member of the committee for public defense. He may become a member of a law enforcement league yet to be formed. He may divorce his wife or elope with his stenographer or misuse the mails and become a Federal prisoner in Leavenworth. Each experience will mean a new role with new personal attitudes and a new axiological conception of himself.[18]

This is none the less illuminating because Babbitt is not the product of a controlled scientific induction. He is a sort of "alleged" symbol which works very well in a psychological equation. Surely, it is enlightening to know that some men are like Babbitt and others like Hamlet, or that we all have our Babbitt and Hamlet phases. But here we should be primarily interested in the fact that the Lynds' *Middletown* (1929) followed rather than preceded Lewis's *Main Street* (1920). In the best of literary and sociological worlds, *Main Street* directs attention to Middletown, and *Middletown* reduces Main Street to an operable entity.

The task of taking language away from poetry is a larger operation than appears at first, and in the eyes of some students an impossible one, even if it were desirable. We are all like Emerson's scholar in that the ordinary affairs of life come to us business and go from us poetry—at least as soon as we start expressing them in speech. Many words which we think of as prosaic literalisms can be shown to have their origin in long-forgotten comparisons. The word "depend" analogizes

18. "The Nature of Human Nature," *American Journal of Sociology*, XXXII (July, 1926), 17.

the action of hanging from; "contact" analogizes a relationship. "Discoverer" and "detect" stand for the literal operation of taking off a covering, hence exposing to view. A "profound study" apparently goes back to our perception of physical depth. In this way the meaning which we attach to these words is transferred from their analogues; and, of course, the process is more obvious in language that is more consciously metaphorical. It thus becomes plain that somewhere one has to come to terms with metaphor anyhow, and there is a way to turn the necessity into a victory.

V

Is the expression of social science affected by a caste spirit? The fact that social scientists are, in general, dedicated to the removal of caste, or at least to a refutation of caste presumptions, unfortunately does not prevent their becoming a caste. Circumstances exist all the while to make them an *élite*. For one thing, the scientific method of procedure sets them off pretty severely from the average man, with his common-sense approach to social problems. Not only is he likely to be nonplussed by techniques and terminologies; he is also likely to be repelled by what scientists consider one of their greatest virtues—their detachment. Finally, it has to be admitted that social scientists' extensive patronage by universities, foundations, and governments serves to give them a protected status while they work. Every other group so situated has tended to create a jargon, and thus far the social scientists have not been an exception. Their jargon is a product partly of imitation and partly of defense-mindedness.

Naturally one of the first steps in entering a profession is to master the professional language. A display of familiarity with the language is popularly taken as a sign of orthodoxy and acceptance; and thus there arises a temptation to use the special nomenclature freely even when one has doubts about its aptness. This condition affects especially the young ones who are seeking recognition and establishment—the graduate students and the instructors—in general, the probationers in the field. Departure from orthodoxy can be interpreted as a sign of ignorance or as a sign of independence, and, in the case of those who have not passed probation, we usually interpret it as the former. Accordingly, there is a degree of risk involved in changing the pattern of speech laid down by one's colleagues. So the problem of what one has to do to show that one belongs can be a problem of style. It is entirely possible that many young social scientists do not write so well as they could because of this inhibition. They are in the position of having to satisfy teachers and critics, and they produce what is expected or what they think is expected. In this way a natural gift for the direct phrase and the lucid arrangement can be swallowed up in tortuosities. The pattern can be broken only by some gifted revolutionary or by someone invested with all the honors of the guild.

It is, moreover, true, as Harold Laski has pointed out, that every profession builds up a distrust of innovation, and especially of innovation from the outside.[19] It requires an unusual degree of humility to see that the solution to our problem may have to come from someone outside our number, perhaps from some naïve person whose advantage is that he can see the matter only in broad outline. Professions and bureaucracies are on guard against this sort of person, and one of the barriers they unconsciously set up is just this one of jargon. If certain government policies were announced in the language of the barbershop, their absurdity might become overwhelmingly apparent. If certain projects in social science research (or in language and literature research, for that matter) were explained in the language of the daily news report, their futility might become embarrassingly clear. One can only surmise how an experienced political reporter would phrase the find-

19. "The Limitations of the Expert," *Harper's*, CLXII (December, 1930), 102–3.

ings in Beyle's *Identification and Analysis of Attribute-Cluster-Blocs*, but one has a notion that his account would sound very little like the original. Would it be unfair? The reply that such language would destroy essential meanings in the original would have to be weighed along with the alternative possibility that the language was used in the first place because it was euphemistic, in the sense we have outlined, or protective. A user of such language may feel safe because the definition of terms is, in a way, his possession. And so technical language, as sometimes employed, may be Pickwickian, inasmuch as it serves not just scientifically but also pragmatically. The average citizen, faced with sociological explanations and bureaucratic communiques, may feel as poor culprits used to feel when confronted with law Latin.

VI

The rhetorical obligation of the scientists has been aptly expressed by T. Swann Harding in a discussion of the general character of scientific writing. "Scientists," he says, "gain nothing by showing off, and the simpler they can make their reports the better. Even their technical reports can be made very much simpler without loss of accuracy or precision. Nor is there really any valid substitute for a good working knowledge of English composition and rhetoric."[20] The last statement is true with certain qualifications, which ought to be made explicit. In a final estimate of the problem it has to be recognized that social science writing cannot be judged altogether by literary standards. It is expression with a definite assignment of duty; and those who have made a comparative study of methods and styles know that every formula of expression incurs its penalty. It is a rule in the realm of writing that one pays for the choice one makes. The payment is exacted when the form of expression becomes too exclusively what it is. In course of use a defined style becomes its own enemy.

20. "The Sad Estate of Scientific Publication," *American Journal of Sociology*, XLVII (January, 1942), 600.

If one's writing is abstract, it will accommodate ideas, but it will fatigue the reader. If it is concrete, it will divert and relieve; but it may become cloying, and it will have difficulty in encompassing ideas. If it is spare, it will come to seem abrupt; if it practices a degree of circumlocution, it will first seem elegant but will come to seem inflated. The lucid style is suspected of oversimplifying. And so the dilemma goes.

Now the social scientist has to write about a kind of thing, and, notwithstanding his uncertain allocation of facts and concepts, he may as well accept his penalty at the beginning. He can never make it a primary goal to be "pleasing," and for this reason the purely literary performance is not for him. Dramatistic presentation, a leading source of interest in all literary production, is largely, if not entirely, out of his reach. The only kind of writing that gets people emotionally involved contains some form of dramatic conflict, which requires a dichotomy of opposites. Yet the only dichotomy that social science (as a science) contemplates is that of the norm and the deviate, and these two are supposed to exist in an empirical rather than in a moral context, and the injunction is implicit that all we shall do is observe. The work, then, is going to be either purely descriptive, or critical with reference to the norm-deviate opposition. Not many people are going to develop a sense of poignant concern over such presentations. To a certain extent *Middletown* did catch the popular imagination, but the contrast developed here was between what the American observably was through the eyes of detached social scientists and his picture of himself, with its compound of self-esteem, aspiration, and social mythology. The community empirically found was put on the stage to challenge the community sentimentally and otherwise conceived. The same will hardly hold for the typical case of scientific norm and empirically discovered deviate, for no such ideas are involved in the contrast. *Recent Social Trends in the United States,*[21] for example, the monumental report of President Hoover's Research Com-

---

21. (2 vols.; New York, 1933.)

mittee on Social Trends, could not look to this kind of interest for its appeal. Unless, therefore, we regard metaphor as a means of dramatistic presentation, this resource is not ordinarily open to social science.

Yet within the purpose which the social scientist sets himself there is a considerable range of rhetorical possibility, which he ignores at needless expense. Rhetoric is, among other things, a process of coordination and subordination which is very close to the essential thought process. That is to say, in any coherent piece of discourse there occur promotion and demotion of thoughts, and this is accomplished not solely through logical outlining and subsumation. It involves matters of sequence, of quantity, and some understanding of the rhetorical aspects of grammatical categories. These are means to clear and effective expression, and the failure to see and use them as means can produce a condition in which means and ends seem not discriminated, or even a subversion in which means seem to manipulate ends. That condition is one which social science, along with every other instrumentality of education, should be combating in the interest of a reasonable world.

Chapter IX

ULTIMATE TERMS
IN CONTEMPORARY RHETORIC

W E HAVE shown that rhetorical force must be conceived as a power transmitted through the links of a chain that extends upward toward some ultimate source. The higher links of that chain must always be of unique interest to the student of rhetoric, pointing, as they do, to some prime mover of human impulse. Here I propose to turn away from general considerations and to make an empirical study of the terms on these higher levels of force which are seen to be operating in our age.

We shall define term simply here as a name capable of entering into a proposition. In our treatment of rhetorical sources, we have regarded the full predication consisting of a proposition as the true validator. But a single term is an incipient proposition, awaiting only the necessary coupling with another term; and it cannot be denied that single names set up expectancies of propositional embodiment. This causes everyone to realize the critical nature of the process of naming. Given the name "patriot," for example, we might expect to see coupled with it "Brutus," or "Washington," or "Parnell"; given the term "hot," we might expect to see "sun," "stove," and so on. In sum, single terms have their potencies, this being part of the phenomenon of names, and we shall here present a few of the most noteworthy in our time, with some remarks upon their etiology.

Naturally this survey will include the "bad" terms as well

as the "good" terms, since we are interested to record historically those expressions to which the populace, in its actual
usage and response, appears to attribute the greatest sanction.
A prescriptive rhetoric may specify those terms which, in all
seasons, ought to carry the greatest potency, but since the
affections of one age are frequently a source of wonder to
another, the most we can do under the caption "contemporary
rhetoric" is to give a descriptive account and withhold the
moral until the end. For despite the variations of fashion, an
age which is not simply distraught manages to achieve some
system of relationship among the attractive and among the
repulsive terms, so that we can work out an order of weight
and precedence in the prevailing rhetoric once we have discerned the "rhetorical absolutes"—the terms to which the very
highest respect is paid.

It is best to begin boldly by asking ourselves, what is the
"god term" of the present age? By "god term" we mean that
expression about which all other expressions are ranked as
subordinate and serving dominations and powers. Its force
imparts to the others their lesser degree of force, and fixes the
scale by which degrees of comparison are understood. In the
absence of a strong and evenly diffused religion, there may be
several terms competing for this primacy, so that the question
is not always capable of definite answer. Yet if one has to select
the one term which in our day carries the greatest blessing,
and—to apply a useful test—whose antonym carries the greatest rebuke, one will not go far wrong in naming "progress."
This seems to be the ultimate generator of force flowing down
through many links of ancillary terms. If one can "make it
stick," it will validate almost anything. It would be difficult to
think of any type of person or of any institution which could
not be recommended to the public through the enhancing
power of this word. A politician is urged upon the voters as a
"progressive leader"; a community is proud to style itself
"progressive"; technologies and methodologies claim to the
"progressive"; a peculiar kind of emphasis in modern educa-

tion calls itself "progressive," and so on without limit. There is no word whose power to move is more implicitly trusted than "progressive." But unlike some other words we shall examine in the course of this chapter, its rise to supreme position is not obscure, and it possesses some intelligible referents.

Before going into the story of its elevation, we must prepare ground by noting that it is the nature of the conscious life of man to revolve around some concept of value. So true is this that when the concept is withdrawn, or when it is forced into competition with another concept, the human being suffers an almost intolerable sense of being lost. He has to know where he is in the ideological cosmos in order to coordinate his activities. Probably the greatest cruelty which can be inflicted upon the psychic man is this deprivation of a sense of tendency. Accordingly every age, including those of rudest cultivation, sets up some kind of sign post. In highly cultivated ages, with individuals of exceptional intellectual strength, this may take the form of a metaphysic. But with the ordinary man, even in such advanced ages, it is likely to be some idea abstracted from religion or historical speculation, and made to inhere in a few sensible and immediate examples.

Since the sixteenth century we have tended to accept as inevitable an historical development that takes the form of a changing relationship between ourselves and nature, in which we pass increasingly into the role of master of nature. When I say that this seems inevitable to us, I mean that it seems something so close to what our more religious forebears considered the working of providence that we regard as impiety any disposition to challenge or even suspect it. By a transposition of terms, "progress" becomes the salvation man is placed on earth to work out; and just as there can be no achievement more important than salvation, so there can be no activity more justified in enlisting our sympathy and support than "progress." As our historical sketch would imply, the term began to be used in the sixteenth century in the sense of continuous development or improvement; it reached an apogee in the nineteenth century, amid noisy demonstrations of man's mastery of nature, and now in the twentieth century it keeps its place as one of the least assailable of the "uncontested terms," despite critical doubts in certain philosophic quarters. It is probably the only term which gives to the average American or West European of today a concept of something bigger than himself, which he is socially impelled to accept and even to sacrifice for. This capacity to demand sacrifice is probably the surest indicator of the "god term," for when a term is so sacrosanct that the material goods of this life must be mysteriously rendered up for it, then we feel justified in saying that it is in some sense ultimate. Today no one is startled to hear of a man's sacrificing health or wealth for the "progress" of the community, whereas such sacrifices for other ends may be regarded as self-indulgent or even treasonable. And this is just because "progress" is the coordinator of all socially respectable effort.

Perhaps these observations will help the speaker who would speak against the stream of "progress," or who, on the other hand, would parry some blow aimed at him through the potency of the word, to realize what a momentum he is opposing.

Another word of great rhetorical force which owes its origin to the same historical transformation is "fact." Today's speaker says "It is a fact" with all the gravity and air of finality with which his less secular-minded ancestor would have said "It is the truth."[1] "These are facts"; "Facts tend to show"; and "He knows the facts" will be recognized as common locutions drawing upon the rhetorical resource of this word. The word "fact" went into the ascendent when our system of verification changed during the Renaissance. Prior to that time, the type of conclusion that men felt obligated to accept came either through divine revelation, or through dialectic, which obeys logical law. But these were displaced by the system of

---

1. It is surely worth observing that nowhere in the King James Version of the Bible does the word "fact" occur.

verification through correspondence with physical reality. Since then things have been true only when measurably true, or when susceptible to some kind of quantification. Quite simply, "fact" came to be the touchstone after the truth of speculative inquiry had been replaced by the truth of empirical investigation. Today when the average citizen says "It is a fact" or says that he "knows the facts in the case," he means that he has the kind of knowledge to which all other knowledges must defer. Possibly it should be pointed out that his "facts" are frequently not facts at all in the etymological sense; often they will be deductions several steps removed from simply factual data. Yet the "facts" of his case carry with them this aura of scientific irrefragability, and he will likely regard any questioning of them as sophistry. In his vocabulary a fact is a fact, and all evidence so denominated has the prestige of science.

These last remarks will remind us at once of the strongly rhetorical character of the word "science" itself. If there is good reason for placing "progress" rather than "science" at the top of our series, it is only that the former has more scope, "science" being the methodological tool of "progress." It seems clear, moreover, that "science" owes its present status to an hypostatization. The hypostatized term is one which treats as a substance or a concrete reality that which has only conceptual existence; and every reader will be able to supply numberless illustrations of how "science" is used without any specific referent. Any utterance beginning "Science says" provides one: "Science says there is no difference in brain capacity between the races"; "Science now knows the cause of encephalitis"; "Science says that smoking does not harm the throat." Science is not, as here it would seem to be, a single concrete entity speaking with one authoritative voice. Behind these large abstractions (and this is not an argument against abstractions as such) there are many scientists holding many different theories and employing many different methods of investigation. The whole force of the word nevertheless de-

pends upon a bland assumption that all scientists meet periodically in synod and there decide and publish what science
believes. Yet anyone with the slightest scientific training
knows that this is very far from a possibility. Let us consider
therefore the changed quality of the utterance when it is
amended to read "A majority of scientists say"; or "Many
scientists believe"; or "Some scientific experiments have indicated." The change will not do. There has to be a creature
called "science"; and its creation has as a matter of practice
been easy, because modern man has been conditioned to believe that the powers and processes which have transformed
his material world represent a very sure form of knowledge,
and that there must be a way of identifying that knowledge.
Obviously the rhetorical aggrandizement of "science" here
parallels that of "fact," the one representing generally and the
other specifically the whole subject matter of trustworthy
perception.

Furthermore, the term "science" like "progress" seems to
satisfy a primal need. Man feels lost without a touchstone of
knowledge just as he feels lost without the direction-finder
provided by progress. It is curious to note that actually the
word is only another name for knowledge (L. *scientia*), so
that if we should go by strict etymology, we should insist that
the expression "science knows" (*i.e.*, "knowledge knows") is
pure tautology. But our rhetoric seems to get around this by
implying that science is *the* knowledge. Other knowledges
may contain elements of quackery, and may reflect the selfish
aims of the knower; but "science," once we have given the
word its incorporation, is the undiluted essence of knowledge.
The word as it comes to us then is a little pathetic in its appeal,
inasmuch as it reflects the deeply human feeling that somewhere somehow there must be people who know things "as
they are." Once God or his ministry was the depository of such
knowledge, but now, with the general decay of religious
faith, it is the scientists who must speak *ex cathedra*, whether
they wish to or not.

The term "modern" shares in the rhetorical forces of the others thus far discussed, and stands not far below the top. Its place in the general ordering is intelligible through the same history. Where progress is real, there is a natural presumption that the latest will be the best. Hence it is generally thought that to describe anything as "modern" is to credit it with all the improvements which have been made up to now. Then by a transference the term is applied to realms where valuation is, or ought to be, of a different source. In consequence, we have "modern living" urged upon us as an ideal; "the modern mind" is mentioned as something superior to previous minds; sometimes the modifier stands alone as an epithet of approval: "to become modern" or "to sound modern" are expressions that carry valuation. It is of course idle not to expect an age to feel that some of its ways and habits of mind are the best; but the extensive transformations of the past hundred years seem to have given "modern" a much more decisive meaning. It is as if a difference of degree had changed into a difference of kind. But the very fact that a word is not used very analytically may increase its rhetorical potency, as we shall see later in connection with a special group of terms.

Another word definitely high up in the hierarchy we have outlined is "efficient." It seems to have acquired its force through a kind of no-nonsense connotation. If a thing is efficient, it is a good adaptation of means to ends, with small loss through friction. Thus as a word expressing a good understanding and management of cause and effect, it may have a fairly definite referent; but when it is lifted above this and made to serve as a term of general endorsement, we have to be on our guard against the stratagems of evil rhetoric. When we find, to cite a familiar example, the phrase "efficiency apartments" used to give an attractive aspect to inadequate dwellings, we may suspect the motive behind such juxtaposition. In many similar cases, "efficient," which is a term above reproach in engineering and physics, is made to hold our attention where ethical and aesthetic considerations are entitled to priority. Certain notorious forms of government and certain brutal forms of warfare are undeniably efficient; but here the featuring of efficiency unfairly narrows the question.

Another term which might seem to have a different provenance but which participates in the impulse we have been studying is "American." One must first recognize the element of national egotism which makes this a word of approval with us, but there are reasons for saying that the force of "American" is much more broadly based than this. "This is the American way" or "It is the American thing to do" are expressions whose intent will not seem at all curious to the average American. Now the peculiar effect that is intended here comes from the circumstance that "American" and "progressive" have an area of synonymity. The Western World has long stood as a symbol for the future; and accordingly there has been a very wide tendency in this country, and also I believe among many people in Europe, to identify that which is American with that which is destined to be. And this is much the same as identifying it with the achievements of "progress." The typical American is quite fatuous in this regard: to him America is the goal toward which all creation moves; and he judges a country's civilization by its resemblance to the American model. The matter of changing nationalities brings out this point very well. For a citizen of a European country to become a citizen of the United States is considered natural and right, and I have known those so transferring their nationality to be congratulated upon their good sense and their anticipated good fortune. On the contrary, when an American takes out British citizenship (French or German would be worse), this transference is felt to be a little scandalous. It is regarded as somehow perverse, or as going against the stream of things. Even some of our intellectuals grow uneasy over the action of Henry James and T. S. Eliot, and the masses cannot comprehend it at all. Their adoption of British citizenship is not mere defection from a country; it is treason to history. If Americans wish to become Europeans, what has happened to the hope of the world? is, I imagine, the question at the back of their minds. The tremendous spread of American fashions in behavior and entertainment must add something to the impetus, but I believe the original source to be this prior idea that America, typifying "progress," is what the remainder of the world is trying to be like.

It follows naturally that in the popular consciousness of this country, "un-American" is the ultimate in negation. An anecdote will serve to illustrate this. Several years ago a leading cigarette manufacturer in this country had reason to believe that very damaging reports were being circulated about his product. The reports were such that had they not been stopped, the sale of this brand of cigarettes might have been reduced. The company thereupon inaugurated an extensive advertising campaign, the object of which was to halt these rumors in the most effective way possible. The concocters of the advertising copy evidently concluded after due deliberation that the strongest term of condemnation which could be conceived was "un-American," for this was the term employed in the campaign. Soon the newspapers were filled with advertising rebuking this "un-American" type of depreciation which had injured their sales. From examples such as this we may infer that "American" stands not only for what is forward in history, but also for what is ethically superior, or at least for a standard of fairness not matched by other nations.

And as long as the popular mind carries this impression, it will be futile to protest against such titles as "The Committee on un-American activities." While "American" and "un-American" continue to stand for these polar distinctions, the average citizen is not going to find much wrong with a group set up to investigate what is "un-American" and therefore reprehensible. At the same time, however, it would strike him as most droll if the British were to set up a "Committee on un-British Activities" or the French a "Committee on un-French Activities." The American, like other nationals, is not apt to be much better than he has been taught, and he has been taught systematically that his country is a special creation. That is why some of his ultimate terms seem to the general view provincial, and why he may be moved to polarities which represent only local poles.

If we look within the area covered by "American," however, we find significant changes in the position of terms which are reflections of cultural and ideological changes. Among the once powerful but now waning terms are those expressive of the pioneer ideal of ruggedness and self-sufficiency. In the space of fifty years or less we have seen the phrase "two-fisted American" pass from the category of highly effective images to that of comic anachronisms. Generally, whoever talks the older language of strenuosity is regarded as a reactionary, it being assumed by social democrats that a socially organized world is one in which cooperation removes the necessity for struggle. Even the rhetorical trump cards of the 1920's, which Sinclair Lewis treated with such satire, are comparatively impotent today, as the new social consciousness causes terms of centrally planned living to move toward the head of the series.

Other terms not necessarily connected with the American story have passed a zenith of influence and are in decline; of these perhaps the once effective "history" is the most interesting example. It is still to be met in such expressions as "History proves" and "History teaches"; yet one feels that it has lost the force it possessed in the previous century. Then it was easy for Byron—"the orator in poetry"—to write, "History with all her volumes vast has but one page"; or for the commemorative speaker to deduce profound lessons from history. But people today seem not to find history so eloquent. A likely explanation is that history, taken as whole, is conceptual rather than factual, and therefore a skepticism has developed as to what it teaches. Moreover, since the teachings of history are principally moral, ethical, or religious, they must encounter today that threshold resentment of anything which savors of the prescriptive. Since "history" is inseparable from judgment of historical fact, there has to be a considerable community of mind before history can be allowed to have a voice. Did the overthrow of Napoleon represent "progress" in history or the reverse? I should say that the most common rhetorical uses of "history" at the present are by intellectuals, whose personal philosophy can provide it with some kind of definition, and by journalists, who seem to use it unreflectively. For the contemporary masses it is substantially true that "history is bunk."

An instructive example of how a coveted term can be monopolized may be seen in "allies." Three times within the memory of those still young, "allies" (often capitalized) has been used to distinguish those fighting on our side from the enemy. During the First World War it was a supreme term; during the Second World War it was again used with effect; and at the time of the present writing it is being used to designate that nondescript combination fighting in the name of the United Nations in Korea. The curious fact about the use of this term is that in each case the enemy also has been constituted of "allies." In the First World War Germany, Austria-Hungary, and Turkey were "allies"; in the Second, Germany and Italy; and in the present conflict the North Koreans and the Chinese and perhaps the Russians are "allies." But in the rhetorical situation it is not possible to refer to them as "allies," since we reserve that term for the alliance representing our side. The reason for such restriction is that when men or nations are "allied," it is implied that they are united on some sound principle or for some good cause. Lying at the source of this feeling is the principle discussed by Plato, that friendship can exist only among the good, since good is an integrating force and evil a disintegrating one. We do not, for example, refer to a band of thieves as "the allies" because that term would impute laudable motives. By confining the term to our side we make an evaluation in our favor. We thus style ourselves the group joined for purposes of good. If we should allow it to be felt for a moment that the opposed combination is also made up of allies, we should concede that they are united by a principle, which in war is never done. So as the usage goes, we are always allies in war and the enemy is just the enemy, regardless of how many nations he has been able to confederate. Here is clearly another instance of how tendencies may exist in even the most innocent-seeming language.

Now let us turn to the terms of repulsion. Some terms of repulsion are also ultimate in the sense of standing at the end of the series, and no survey of the vocabulary can ignore these prime repellants. The counterpart of the "god term" is the "devil term," and it has already been suggested that with us "un-American" comes nearest to filling that role. Sometimes, however, currents of politics and popular feeling cause something more specific to be placed in that position. There seems indeed to be some obscure psychic law which compels every nation to have in its national imagination an enemy. Perhaps this is but a version of the tribal need for a scapegoat, or for something which will personify "the adversary." If a nation did not have an enemy, an enemy would have to be invented to take care of those expressions of scorn and hatred to which peoples must give vent. When another political state is not available to receive the discharge of such emotions, then a class will be chosen, or a race, or a type, or a political faction, and this will be held up to a practically standardized form of repudiation. Perhaps the truth is that we need the enemy in order to define ourselves, but I will not here venture further into psychological complexities. In this type of study it will be enough to recall that during the first half century of our nation's existence, "Tory" was such a devil term. In the period following our Civil War, "rebel" took its place in the Northern section and "Yankee" in the Southern, although in the previous epoch both of these had been terms of esteem. Most readers will remember that during the First World War "pro-German" was a term of destructive force. During the Second World War "Nazi" and "Fascist" carried about equal power to condemn, and then, following the breach with Russia, "Communist" displaced them both. Now "Communist" is beyond any rival the devil term, and as such it is employed even by the American president when he feels the need of a strong rhetorical point.

A singular truth about these terms is that, unlike several which were examined in our favorable list, they defy any real analysis. That is to say, one cannot explain how they generate their peculiar force of repudiation. One only recognizes them as publicly-agreed-upon devil terms. It is the same with all. "Tory" persists in use, though it has long lost any connection with redcoats and British domination. Analysis of "rebel" and "Yankee" only turns up embarrassing contradictions of position. Similarly we have all seen "Nazi" and "Fascist" used without rational perception; and we see this now, in even greater degree, with "Communist." However one might like to reject such usage as mere ignorance, to do so would only evade a very important problem. Most likely these are instances of the "charismatic term," which will be discussed in detail presently.

No student of contemporary usage can be unmindful of the curious reprobative force which has been acquired by the term "prejudice." Etymologically it signifies nothing more than a prejudgment, or a judgment before all the facts are in; and since all of us have to proceed to a great extent on judgments of that kind, the word should not be any more exciting than "hypothesis." But in its rhetorical applications "prejudice" presumes far beyond that. It is used, as a matter of fact, to characterize unfavorably any value judgment whatever. If "blue" is said to be a better color than "red," that is prejudice. If people of outstanding cultural achievement are praised through contrast with another people, that is prejudice. If one mode of life is presented as superior to another, that is prejudice. And behind all is the implication, if not the declaration, that it is un-American to be prejudiced.

I suspect that what the users of this term are attempting, whether consciously or not, is to sneak "prejudiced" forward as an uncontested term, and in this way to disarm the opposition by making all positional judgments reprehensible. It must be observed in passing that no people are so prejudiced in the sense of being committed to valuations as those who are engaged in castigating others for prejudice. What they expect is that they can nullify the prejudices of those who oppose them, and then get their own installed in the guise of the *sensus communis*. Mark Twain's statement, "I know that I am prejudiced in this matter, but I would be ashamed of myself if I weren't" is a therapeutic insight into the process; but it will take more than a witticism to make headway against the repulsive force gathered behind "prejudice."

If the rhetorical use of the term has any rational content, this probably comes through a chain of deductions from the nature of democracy; and we know that in controversies centered about the meaning of democracy, the air is usually filled with cries of "prejudice." If democracy is taken crudely to mean equality, as it very frequently is, it is then a contradiction of democracy to assign inferiority and superiority on whatever grounds. But since the whole process of evaluation is a process of such assignment, the various inequalities which are left when it has done its work are contradictions of this root notion and hence are "prejudice"—the assumption of course being that when all the facts are in, these inequalities will be found illusory. The man who dislikes a certain class or race or style has merely not taken pains to learn that it is just as good as any other. If all inequality is deception, then superiorities must be accounted the products of immature judgment. This affords plausible ground, as we have suggested, for the coupling of "prejudice" and "ignorance."

Before leaving the subject of the ordered series of good and bad terms, one feels obliged to say something about the way in which hierarchies can be inverted. Under the impulse of strong frustration there is a natural tendency to institute a pretense that the best is the worst and the worst is the best—an inversion sometimes encountered in literature and in social deportment. The best illustration for purpose of study here comes from a department of speech which I shall call "GI rhetoric." The average American youth, put into uniform, translated to a new and usually barren environment, and imbued from many sources with a mission of killing, has undergone a pretty severe dislocation. All of this runs counter to the benevolent platitudes on which he was brought up, and there is little ground for wonder if he adopts the inverted pose. This is made doubly likely by the facts that he is at a passionate age and that he is thrust into an atmosphere of superinduced excitement. It would be unnatural for him not to acquire a rhetoric of strong impulse and of contumacious tendency.

What he does is to make an almost complete inversion. In this special world of his he recoils from those terms used by politicians and other civilians and by the "top brass" when they are enunciating public sentiments. Dropping the conventional terms of attraction, this uprooted and specially focussed young man puts in their place terms of repulsion. To be more specific, where the others use terms reflecting love, hope, and charity, he uses almost exclusively terms connected with the excretory and reproductive functions. Such terms comprise what Kenneth Burke has ingeniously called "the imagery of killing." By an apparently universal psychological law, faeces and the act of defecation are linked with the idea of killing, of destruction, of total repudiation—perhaps the word "elimination" would comprise the whole body of notions. The reproductive act is associated especially with the idea of aggressive exploitation. Consequently when the GI feels that he must give his speech a proper show of spirit, he places the symbols for these things in places which would normally be filled by prestige terms from the "regular" list. For specimens of such language presented in literature, the reader is referred to the fiction of Ernest Hemingway and Norman Mailer.

Anyone who has been compelled to listen to such rhetoric will recall the monotony of the vocabulary and the vehemence of the delivery. From these two characteristics we may infer a great need and a narrow means of satisfaction, together with the tension which must result from maintaining so arduous an inversion. Whereas previously the aim had been to love (in the broad sense) it is now to kill; whereas it had been freedom and individuality, it is now restriction and brutalization. In taking revenge for a change which so contradicts his upbringing he is quite capable, as the evidence has already proved, of defiantly placing the lower level above the higher. Sometimes a clever GI will invent combinations and will effect metaphorical departures, but the ordinary ones are limited to a reiteration of the stock terms—to a reiteration, with emphasis of intonation, upon "the imagery of killing."[2] Taken as a whole, this rhetoric is a clear if limited example of how the machine may be put in reverse—of how, consequently, a sort of devil worship may get into language.

A similar inversion of hierarchy is to be seen in the world of competitive sports, although to a lesser extent. The great majority of us in the Western world have been brought up under the influence, direct or indirect, of Christianity, which is a religion of extreme altruism. Its terms of value all derive from a law of self-effacement and of consideration for others, and these terms tend to appear whenever we try to rationalize or vindicate our conduct. But in the world of competitive sports, the direction is opposite: there one is applauded for egotistic display and for success at the expense of others—should one mention in particular American professional baseball? Thus the terms with which an athlete is commended will generally point away from the direction of Christian passivity,

---

2. Compare Sherwood Anderson's analysis of the same phenomenon in *A Story Teller's Story* (New York, 1928), p. 198: "There was in the factories where I worked and where the efficient Ford type of man was just beginning his dull reign this strange and futile outpouring of men's lives in vileness through their lips. Ennui was at work. The talk of the men about me was not Rabelaisian. In old Rabelais there was the salt of infinite wit and I have no doubt that the Rabelaisian flashes that came from our own Lincoln, Washington, and others had point and a flare to them.

But in the factories and in army camps!"

although when an athlete's character is described for the benefit of the general public, some way is usually found to place him in the other ethos, as by calling attention to his natural kindness, his interest in children, or his readiness to share his money.

Certainly many of the contradictions of our conduct may be explained through the presence of these small inverted hierarchies. When, to cite one further familiar example, the acquisitive, hard-driving local capitalist is made the chief lay official of a Christian church, one knows that in a definite area there has been a transvaluation of values.

Earlier in the chapter we referred to terms of considerable potency whose referents it is virtually impossible to discover or to construct through imagination. I shall approach this group by calling them "charismatic terms." It is the nature of the charismatic term to have a power which is not derived, but which is in some mysterious way given. By this I mean to say that we cannot explain their compulsiveness through referents of objectively known character and tendency. We normally "understand" a rhetorical term's appeal through its connection with something we apprehend, even when we object morally to the source of the impulse. Now "progress" is an understandable term in this sense, since it rests upon certain observable if not always commendable aspects of our world. Likewise the referential support of "fact" needs no demonstrating. These derive their force from a reading of palpable circumstance. But in charismatic terms we are confronted with a different creation: these terms seem to have broken loose somehow and to operate independently of referential connections (although in some instances an earlier history of referential connection may be made out). Their meaning seems inexplicable unless we accept the hypothesis that their content proceeds out of a popular will that they *shall* mean something. In effect, they are rhetorical by common consent, or by "charisma." As is the case with charismatic authority, where the populace gives the leader a power which can by no means be explained through his personal attributes, and permits him to use it effectively and even arrogantly, the charismatic term is given its load of impulsion without reference, and it functions by convention. The number of such terms is small in any one period, but they are perhaps the most efficacious terms of all.

Such rhetorical sensibility as I have leads me to believe that one of the principal charismatic terms of our age is "freedom." The greatest sacrifices that contemporary man is called upon to make are demanded in the name of "freedom"; yet the referent which the average man attaches to this word is most obscure. Burke's dictum that "freedom inheres in something sensible" has not prevented its breaking loose from all anchorages. And the evident truth that the average man, given a choice between exemption from responsibility and responsibility, will choose the latter, makes no impression against its power. The fact, moreover, that the most extensive use of the term is made by modern politicians and statesmen in an effort to get men to assume more responsibility (in the form of military service, increased taxes, abridgement of rights, etc.) seems to carry no weight either.[3] The fact that what the American pioneer considered freedom has become wholly impossible to the modern apartment-dwelling metropolitan seems not to have damaged its potency. Unless we accept some philosophical interpretation, such as the proposition that freedom consists only in the discharge of responsibility, there seems no possibility of a correlation between the use of the word and circumstantial reality. Yet "freedom" remains an ultimate term, for which people are asked to yield up their first-born.

There is plenty of evidence that "democracy" is becoming the same kind of term. The variety of things it is used to symbolize is too weird and too contradictory for one to find even a core meaning in present-day usages. More important

---

3. One is inevitably reminded of the slogan of Oceania in Orwell's *Nineteen Eighty-four:* "Freedom is Slavery."

than this for us is the fact, noted by George Orwell, that people resist any attempt to define democracy, as if to connect it with a clear and fixed referent were to vitiate it. It may well be that such resistance to definition of democracy arises from a subconscious fear that a term defined in the usual manner has its charisma taken away. The situation then is that "democracy" means "be democratic," and that means exhibit a certain attitude which you can learn by imitating your fellows.

If rationality is measured by correlations and by analyzable content, then these terms are irrational; and there is one further modern development in the creation of such terms which is strongly suggestive of irrational impulse. This is the increasing tendency to employ in the place of the term itself an abbreviated or telescoped form—which form is nearly always used with even more reckless assumption of authority. I seldom read the abbreviation "U S" in the newspapers without wincing at the complete arrogance of its rhetorical tone. Daily we see "U S Cracks Down on Communists"; "U S Gives OK to Atomic Weapons"; "U S Shocked by Death of Official." Who or what is this "U S"? It is clear that "U S" does not suggest a union of forty-eight states having republican forms of government and held together by a constitution of expressly delimited authority. It suggests rather an abstract force out of a new world of forces, whose will is law and whom the individual citizen has no way to placate. Consider the individual citizen confronted by "U S" or "FBI." As long as terms stand for identifiable organs of government, the citizen feels that he knows the world he moves around in, but when the forces of government are referred to by these bloodless abstractions, he cannot avoid feeling that they are one thing and he another. Let us note while dealing with this subject the enormous proliferation of such forms during the past twenty years or so. If "U S" is the most powerful and prepossessing of the group, it drags behind it in train the previously mentioned "FBI," and "NPA," "ERP," "FDIC," "WPA," "HOLC," and "OSS," to take a few at random. It is a fact of ominous significance that this use of foreshortened forms is preferred by totalitarians, both the professed and the disguised. Americans were hearing the terms "OGPU," "AMTORG" and "NEP" before their own government turned to large-scale state planning. Since then we have spawned them ourselves, and, it is to be feared, out of similar impulse. George Orwell, one of the truest humanists of our age, has described the phenomenon thus: "Even in the early decades of the twentieth century, telescoped words and phrases had been one of the characteristic features of political language; and it had been noticed that the tendency to use abbreviations of this kind was most marked in totalitarian countries and totalitarian organizations. Examples were such words as Nazi, Gestapo, Comintern, Inprecor, Agitprop."[4]

I venture to suggest that what this whole trend indicates is an attempt by the government, as distinguished from the people, to confer charismatic authority. In the earlier specimens of charismatic terms we were examining, we beheld something like the creation of a spontaneous general will. But these later ones of truncated form are handed down from above, and their potency is by fiat of whatever group is administering in the name of democracy. Actually the process is no more anomalous than the issuing of pamphlets to soldiers telling them whom they shall hate and whom they shall like (or try to like), but the whole business of switching impulse on and off from a central headquarters has very much the meaning of *Gleichschaltung* as that word has been interpreted for me by a native German. Yet it is a disturbing fact that such process should increase in times of peace, because the persistent use of such abbreviations can only mean a serious divorce between rhetorical impulse and rational thought. When the ultimate terms become a series of bare abstractions, the understanding of power is supplanted by a worship of power, and in our condition this can mean only state worship.

It is easy to see, however, that a group determined upon control will have as one of its first objectives the appropriation

----

4. "Principles of Newspeak," *Nineteen Eighty-four* (New York, 1949), p. 310.

of sources of charismatic authority. Probably the surest way to detect the fabricated charismatic term is to identify those terms ordinarily of limited power which are being moved up to the front line. That is to say, we may suspect the act of fabrication when terms of secondary or even tertiary rhetorical rank are pushed forward by unnatural pressure into ultimate positions. This process can nearly always be observed in times of crisis. During the last war, for example, "defense" and "war effort" were certainly regarded as culminative terms. We may say this because almost no one thinks of these terms as the natural sanctions of his mode of life. He may think thus of "progress" or "happiness" or even "freedom"; but "defense" and "war effort" are ultimate sanctions only when measured against an emergency situation. When the United States was preparing for entry into that conflict, every departure from our normal way of life could be justified as a "defense" measure. Plants making bombs to be dropped on other continents were called "defense" plants. Correspondingly, once the conflict had been entered, everything that was done in military or civilian areas was judged by its contribution to the "war effort." This last became for a period of years the supreme term: not God or Heaven or happiness, but successful effort in the war. It was a term to end all other terms or a rhetoric to silence all other rhetoric. No one was able to make his claim heard against "the war effort."

It is most important to realize, therefore, that under the stress of feeling or preoccupation, quite secondary terms can be moved up to the position of ultimate terms, where they will remain until reflection is allowed to resume sway. There are many signs to show that the term "aggressor" is now undergoing such manipulation. Despite the fact that almost no term is more difficult to correlate with objective phenomena, it is being rapidly promoted to ultimate "bad" term. The likelihood is that "aggressor" will soon become a depository for all the resentments and fears which naturally arise in a people. As such, it will function as did "infidel" in the mediaeval period and as "reactionary" has functioned in the recent past. Manifestly it is of great advantage to a nation bent upon organizing its power to be able to stigmatize some neighbor as "aggressor," so that the term's capacity for irrational assumption is a great temptation for those who are not moral in their use of rhetoric. This passage from natural or popular to state-engendered charisma produces one of the most dangerous lesions of modern society.

An ethics of rhetoric requires that ultimate terms be ultimate in some rational sense. The only way to achieve that objective is through an ordering of our own minds and our own passions. Every one of psychological sophistication knows that there is a pleasure in willed perversity, and the setting up of perverse shibboleths is a fairly common source of that pleasure. War cries, school slogans, coterie passwords, and all similar expressions are examples of such creation. There may be areas of play in which these are nothing more than a diversion; but there are other areas in which such expressions lure us down the roads of hatred and tragedy. That is the tendency of all words of false or "engineered" charisma. They often sound like the very gospel of one's society, but in fact they betray us; they get us to do what the adversary of the human being wants us to do. It is worth considering whether the real civil disobedience must not begin with our language.

Lastly, the student of rhetoric must realize that in the contemporary world he is confronted not only by evil practitioners, but also, and probably to an unprecedented degree, by men who are conditioned by the evil created by others. The machinery of propagation and inculcation is today so immense that no one avoids entirely the assimilation and use of some terms which have a downward tendency. It is especially easy to pick up a tone without realizing its trend. Perhaps the best that any of us can do is to hold a dialectic with himself to see what the wider circumferences of his terms of persuasion are. This process will not only improve the consistency of one's thinking but it will also, if the foregoing analysis is sound, prevent his becoming a creature of evil public forces and a victim of his own thoughtless rhetoric.

Index